VLADIVOSTOK

Acknowledgements

Macmillan and Co.

Faber

Dolmen Press

Benziger of Zurich

The Irish Times

David Marcus and The Irish Press

Jonathan Williams

RTE Radio

and many defunct Irish literary
magazines of the 1940s and 1950s

VLADIVOSTOK

Maurice Kennedy

Foreword by Augustine Martin

The Way To Vladivostok
Second Edition, 2020
Published by
Tara Press, Dublin

First published 2000
by Val Mulkerns
Dublin

ISBN: 978-1-9999262-3-6

Cover image: Mihai Barboo

Frontspiece, Vladivostock: this image is the original pen and ink art work that accompanied one published version of the title story, possibly in the British edition of *Winter's Tales*. Unfortunately, the name of the illustrator is unknown.

Author image: the portrait at the back of the book was taken by a colleague of the author, whose name is at present unknown. The publisher will happily credit the photographer as soon as it can be found.

I have watched and travelled hard
Sometime I will slepe out, the rest Ile whistle:
A good man's fortune may grow out at heels.
Give you good morrow.

(King Lear: Kent.)
Act II Sc. II

FOREWORD

When asked by Val Mulkerns to edit a selection of her late husband's work I felt quite complex emotions: pride at being asked, nostalgia for a lean but rigorous time in Irish writing, mild terror at handling the reputation of a man who had such high standards and retiring ways. When I agreed, and when the nerves settled, I felt the difficulty of balancing the shyness of his personality, and the deliberate spareness of his canon against the duty of showing him to best advantage – his dark humour and unsentimental lyricism, those remarkable flashes of poetry amid the spare precision of his prose:

> *The street was deserted, except for the carpenter, who had a long baulk of timber propped against the front of his shed, and was trimming it for use as a cart-shaft; he looked small in the distance, but we could see the movement of the adze, and the flash of sunlight from the blade as it paused at the top of its swing, then the streak of light as it fell swiftly. A long time afterwards we heard the dull sound as it bit into the timber, and we stood there for a while listening. Nothing else broke the stillness. The village dogs lay curled in the shadows, fast asleep.*

This is the timeless summer of childhood; yet time is somehow measured by the journey of light and sound, the world authenticated by a timeless human activity.

At the centre of the writer's simplicities there is a deep sophistication, a core of watchful intensity. This is equally true of his deceptively casual journalism and travel pieces in the second half of this volume. As for his literary judgements, they always seem to reach the heart of the matter without flourish or fuss.

Maurice Kennedy was a sort of legend to my generation, in particular to those who graduated from UCD in the mid-fifties and wondered what the next move might be – to write a great novel or slim volume, to publish an aesthetic manifesto or live one by starving in a Parisian garret. So little was happening. *Envoy* had closed down in 1951, *The Bell* in 1954. In that same year *Irish Writing* ceased regular publication with the end of David Marcus's editorship – it maintained a sporadic life under Sean J. White for another couple of years.

Austin Clarke wrote vague mandarin reviews every Saturday for *The Irish Times*. Deep-browed Kavanagh ruled a shadowy demesne in Harry Street with Myles, Tony Cronin, Patrick Swift and John Jordan in attendance: wet-behind-the-ears aspirants approach at peril! Benedict Kiely was unpretentiously accessible around Burgh Quay; Mary Lavin, if you could get an entrée, held court at her mews in Lad Lane – a promising young Leitrim man by the name of McGahern was rumoured to attend.

The Maurice Kennedy legend is based on a single story, intimidatingly entitled 'Vladivostok' (1954). The title was perfect, confirming our impression of the author as a remote and Chekovian genius, redolent of angst and modernity. In the grittily urbane book reviews which he wrote for *The Irish Times* he tended to complain about literary over-production: better not write at all, he seemed to assert, than to write badly or just for the sake of writing. We felt a little threatened by this, but consoled ourselves with the possibility that he might be making an elaborate rationalisation of writer's block. (Surely the author of 'Vladivostok' could not willingly forsake his muse!).

The wry truth of the affair is cheerfully rehearsed in his 'anti-memoir' which opens this book and which he entitles 'The Collected Works'. There amid the authentic whiff of bohemian Dublin in the fifties, with such choice and master spirits as Liam and Seamus Miller, Michael Biggs and Tony Cronin – who sums it up as a world 'full of the smell of money gone' – nothing less momentous than the dubious story by Maurice Kennedy. I won't anticipate the reader's delight by further comment on this strange period piece and its odd companions. For maximum effect I suggest this order of reading: 'The Collected Works', 'Freebooters', 'Vladivostok'. Together they enact an exquisite drama of personal sensibility and the creative process, with Kennedy's shy, deprecating consciousness at their centre.

That superb story, 'Vladivostok' – abridged for Irish Writing in its first published version – seemed slowly to eclipse all other new fiction around 1954. The full version, which appears below, was acclaimed when it came out in the British *Winters Tales* series from Macmillan, and translated into several foreign languages. The brilliant literary career that it promised did not materialise, for reasons that must remain in part mysterious, and are in part rehearsed and clarified in the present volume.

The facts of Maurice Kennedy's life could hardly be less remarkable. He was born in Youghal, County Cork, in 1924 and went to school in Limerick. He studied Science without enthusiasm at UCC and left before graduating to take up an appointment as Examiner of Estate Duties with the Revenue Commissioners. Like so many other Irish literary figures – Mervyn Wall, Brian O'Nolan, Thomas Kinsella – he made a living in the Civil Service, while writing, reviewing and broadcasting in his spare time. But he stayed in the job for forty years.

He married Val Mulkerns in 1953: they had two sons and a daughter. His last years were shadowed by extreme bad health.

Those who knew Maurice Kennedy will speak affectionately of his wit, warmth and learning; reverently of his truth and integrity. I believe that much of his personality is present in this selection of his work which was assembled mostly by his family. While we might wish he had written more, we rejoice that he has written so well.

Augustine Martin
August 1994

Augustine Martin, Professor of Anglo-Irish Literature and Drama, University College Dublin, was born in Leitrim in 1935 and died in Dublin in 1995.

TABLE OF CONTENTS

Part one

FACTION

The Collected Works (an anti-memoir) 15

Part two

FICTION

Neither Virgin Nor Martyr 25
The Heroes 30
A Small Green Hollow Like A Grave 40
Freebooters 49
Vladivostok 59

Part three

EPHEMERA

On a Blue Note 90
Olivermanship 93
George Fitzmaurice (Sketch for a portrait) 96
Wild Strawberries 112
Terribly Strange Beds 115
Cast A Cold Eye 128
The Feast of Oval 133
A Hunting Of The Shark 141
A Little Winter Journey 146

PART I

FACTION

THE COLLECTED WORKS

It was somewhere on the north side. My student daughter was engaged in the usual Saturday night ritual of cadging a lift to some far-flung orgy. I hadn't bothered to find out the name of the place, since I had a navigator, and it didn't seem even remotely familiar at first because suburbs change these days while your back is turned, let alone in twenty years. Something jogged my memory as we turned into a narrow road.

"What is this place?" I said. She told me. "Oh God," I said, "get out quick and get a taxi home." The tyres squealed on the first sharp corner, and I noted with interest that it took me twenty minutes in a fast car, through one way streets and roundabouts, to cover the journey into town that I scheduled at eight and a half minutes on the road-racing bike I used in those blown-away leafmeal days.

"Would that mine enemy had written a book!" said Job. There were two books really, and neither of them was what you could honestly call a book, anyway, and one of them was even less so than the other. If you follow me? No? Well, attend carefully, because this is vital bibliographic stuff, as thrilling as the Decipherment of Linear B.

—~—

Once upon a wet Monday, and a very wet lunch-hour it was to be sure, I was reduced to reading one of the more odious English Sunday papers – which has long since perished to the regret of nobody but its unfortunate staff. In the grip of the insanity that comes over most newspapers at times, it announced a short-story competition with vast prizes. Newspaper competitions do nothing very helpful for a short story, even the print area being inimical to the necessary balance and flow; and the type of Christmas-supplement story that wins newspaper competitions does little for the paper concerned, even if the resounding lack of public interest in the short story hadn't shown its defects as a publicity medium.

I saw no reason to tell the wretched paper how to spend its wretched money, and there was a long blank hour left. So I sharpened a pencil and, stealing briskly from Padraig Colum his romantic image of the ploughman ("around him earth savage, earth broken") began to write a lush bit of slush about tinkers. It flowed turgidly and effortlessly on, like shamrocks stewed in beet-sugar treacle. By the time I ended, with a ring of happy, bronzed faces in the firelight, washing down the stolen goose with great draughts of porter out of Seamus O'Kelly's diamond-notched cans. I'd left hardly a cliché unturned. Man, it was massive.

Not quite massive enough in the literal sense, because a quick inspection that night showed it was a few hundred words too short for the contest. No problem. I cut it apart in convenient places and spliced in a rabbit here, a 'patch of fragrant' peonies elsewhere (oh, the acute, despicable pleasure of that last phrase!). Hopefully I wrapped up the result before my resolution could fail. There was just a chance that this unfamiliar type of nonsense might bamboozle the judges.

It didn't, in fact. As I dimly recall, the competition was won by a story in an equally disreputable tradition, in which a pure-souled prostitute was redeemed by a sort of Christ-figure disguised as a meths-drinker. I bowed to a more cynical master, and threw the manuscript in a drawer for a while.

A year later, on some mad impulse, I sent it to that courteous, old-fashioned gentleman, Seamus O'Sullivan. I'd met him in another connection, and he'd asked me civilly whether I wrote, and it seemed only civil to send him something. But, God help him, he liked it. I doubt whether he'd ever seen a tinker at close quarters (that was a long time before they invaded Dublin) and I suspect he regarded the countryside as something to be walked through rapidly for reasons of exercise or used as a conventional background for Georgian poetry. The story may have carried him back to the great days of the early Abbey, when everybody was carving up great reeking slabs of synthetic Peasant Quality (he had actually carried scenery') for that first production through the old graveyard at the back of the Antient Concert Rooms. "Oh, those tombstones," he said, nibbing his shins reminiscently 50 years later). I'd no such excuse, having grown up immersed to my oxters in PQ, but my confidence in the utterly deplorable nature of the story was temporarily shaken. Perhaps I had accidentally achieved something of intrinsic value, a nugget of genuine bog oak?

I smothered my conscience and let the story come out in *The Dublin Magazine,* where it was seen and praised by various urban critics, who probably liked to think the country was like this. And I accepted my cheque with real gratitude. Those were the hungry '40s which, as Cronin acutely said, were "full of the smell of money gone." On This slender foundation of actual cash, our little theatrical company built a small inverted pyramid of credit that enabled us to put on a long-lost play of genuine Peasant Quality: and even, by some miracle, as in the old puzzle story about the seventeen camels, I emerged at the end with my investment intact.

We had a party on the last night that almost got the Peacock closed forever, but that's another story and I've mercifully forgotten most of it. Some time in the small gin-sodden hours my fellow impresario, who had recently bought a tiny hand-printing press, announced his intention of bringing out my story as a book. At that hour of the morning all sorts of things seem possible and even desirable. In his case, the hangover lasted.

—∾—

A year or so later the joke, as it had seemed, began to take concrete shape in hand-set type on fine thick paper. Big print and a small page area combined to produce some severe problems of justification, but these were easily surmounted. On one occasion I wrote an eleven and a half line sunset that James A. Fitzpatrick would have envied, and again a count of the available spaces dictated a change from chocolate-coloured earth to coffee-coloured ditto. 'The theatre,' as Mary McCarthy said, 'is essentially a pragmatic art.' Little bookmaking likewise.

The "book" was not so much launched as floated out gently from a tiny house in the shadow of the gasometer. Throughout a long and fluid night I signed and numbered copies, and my usual lousy signature became steadily more illegible as writer's cramp set in. Meanwhile the Guinness bottles, a particularly good batch from the Widow's establishment, travelled diagonally across the floor from the store-heap in one corner to the pile of dead men in the other. It was an excellent impromptu party. Nobody got drunk, nobody got maudlin, nobody got aggressive. Peripheral people drifted away at intervals in the small hours, and as the dawn came up over Spencer Dock, a re-examination of the discards produced just enough drinkable stout to wash down the breakfast sausages for the survivors – the Weatherman, the Railwayman, the Sculptor, the Impresario and the Author.* It was the only party in my experience that ever ended so tidily.

There was, in retrospect, a surprising amount of publicity. I came across a bundle of clippings the other day, and they bulked larger than the book itself. We even got reviewed.** Christine, typically Sibylline, said the text had "a certain juvenile charm" but that the book "somewhat lacked ink". Some copies were actually sold, even perhaps to strangers, and a new publishing house was triumphantly established. My sister bought a copy. My colleague in the office actually bought two, possibly to have one pristine copy when he'd worn out the first: I don't know, but the same colleague subsequently lent me his car to drive around Ireland when he knew I hadn't then learned to drive, so his judgement must be suspect.

~

Some years later I wrote a real story and after that forswore fiction. *Waiting for Godot* has been well described as a play

* *The Weatherman was Seamus Miller, the Sculptor Michael Biggs, the Impresario Liam Miller, the Author Maurice Kennedy. Nobody I have encountered can identify The Railwayman. (Editor)*

** *Christine Longford was the reviewer.*

in which nothing happens, twice. In my story nothing happened, once, at quite remarkable length, and I realised this was as far as I could go: no Nobels for me. My friend the Ambassador* decided to include the story in a standard anthology, but before then my friend the Impresario had the notion that it, plus two earlier, slighter pieces would make another nice little volume, more substantial than the first. Matteradamn to me, of course: old friends are welcome to anything. The wild scheme had advanced to the early production stage, and one of the slighter pieces was actually in galley proofs: publication was imminent. Therefore when the Ambassador's anthology appeared, it credited my opus to, among other sources, a volume called *Wanwood*. ("As the heart grows older/It will come to such sights colder...nor spare a sigh/Though worlds of wanwood leafmeal lie.")

The trouble was that *Wanwood* had not appeared as expected, and during the intervening twenty years of hearts growing older and colder it has swum up once towards the surface like a goldfish's ghost and then disappeared forever.

I'd forgotten about the jinx, the hex, the story that had actually been type-set; or perhaps I just hadn't admitted it to myself at that stage, because it's difficult for a totally unsuperstitious person to admit such things. It was an average piece of neo-Bates juvenilia, interesting only in that I'd managed to produce an imitation of Joyce's "Araby" before I'd ever read the original. But a jinx? Nonsense. Yet over the years it had accumulated a clutch of identical rejection slips from reputable magazines, regretting that they would have liked to use it but the next issue was to be

** *The Ambassador was the poet Valentin Iremonger.*

their last. It was of course a period of high mortality in the magazine business, but... And, of course, it was pure coincidence that three successive literary agents, who had agreed to handle the story, died: they were old, I suppose. One friend who had dealings with the manuscript broke and permanently damaged a leg; another merely an ankle. These were just the highlights.

—∾—

It seems ludicrous when I set it down, and I don't expect anybody to believe it, but I was forced eventually to realise that I must have incorporated something out of the Cabala, the verbal equivalent of a virus, a complex of inert matter that activates and becomes lethal only when it meets a potential host. I read the thing several times as my suspicions grew, and could see nothing but a piece of not-good, not-bad fretwork, could see no reason why this particular sequence of unpublished words should ruin friendships and break limbs and kill magazines and people. Clearly, it wasn't worth the risk, however, and hard though it is for even a retired author to do such things, I set about recovering and destroying all the manuscript copies at large.

I had inexplicably forgotten about the aborted *Wanwood* project, though that was obviously another casualty on the list; my memory had played tricks and substituted another story.

A few years later, when the abandoned (as I'd thought) project was mentioned again out of the blue, I came to my senses and ordered that the whole thing be scrubbed, cancelled, retrospectively nullified to avoid disaster. I hope it was.

Of course the idea of *Wanwood* still hangs there like the Cheshire Cat's disembodied smile. A couple of years ago I had an indignant phone-call from a lady who was compiling an official list of Irish writings. Why had she never been able to locate a copy of *Wanwood*? Why was I wasting her valuable time and energy? I don't think she believed my implausible story of an imaginary book, and I hate to think of what she would have said if I mentioned the jinx. I can't remember hearing that the official list ever appeared. For that matter, it occurs to me that my friend the Ambassador is called on to serve his country in the tundra or the tropics instead of the temperate climates which he loves.

—w—

So much for the book that wasn't. But before that we had lived for a while in a rented house, and in a corner of one of the empty rooms there lay the remains of the edition of the little book that was. There was another party before we left, and in the pre-dawn tristia the Impresario and myself were moved by a single splendid thought. Reciting such fragments as we could remember of "The Burial of Sir John Moore at Corunna", with the aid of a bicycle lamp and a coal shovel and a small libation of flat stout, we interred the pile of volumes deep under the virgin builder's rubble of the back garden.

It all came back to me when I turned unexpectedly into that narrow forgotten road. What unspeakable things might be growing in one of those suburban gardens, by now presumably cultivated and mature? Triffids? Worse?

I would prefer not to know.

PART II

FICTION

NEITHER VIRGIN NOR MARTYR

It was damnably hot on that interminably long, interminably straight road that runs from Bologna towards Rimini and the unimaginable Adriatic. Towards sea breezes, cooling even if composed of the inimitable Adriatic sun-oil and diluted sewage. The synthetic shade of a beach umbrella. Something to drink. Something to read. Here the little poplars had gathered their shadows primly around their toes and offered no shelter to anything bigger than a cricket. I might as well sit patiently in the malignant sunlight on a kilometre stone and wait for Fred to turn up with the jeep and all the gear. Surely the bloody thing couldn't have broken down yet again? Or had Fred perhaps been so inflamed by the commercialised Romeo and Julietry of Verona, (where we'd stayed over on our way from climbing in the Dolomites), that he'd said "tu" instead of "lei" to some luscious young lady and had himself knifed by an outraged *fidanzato*? Anyway, whether Fred or the jeep or both had broken down, I wasn't going to walk the ten miles back into Bologna unless I had to.

Meanwhile I had nothing to eat and nothing to drink and nothing to read, although ten miles away there was an icebox in the jeep and a Stendhal in the pocket of my climbing jacket. Damn Fred. A further search of the various pockets in the reliable old bush shirt, not worn since the previous summer, disclosed a forgotten biscuit, most of which promptly crumbled away at my feet. Also the back of a cigarette packet, scribbled with notes that may once have been merely cryptic but were now totally incomprehensible. Also, a baffling page from a Missal, which I stared at for some time before remembering why I'd made a souvenir of it in the first place, doubtless committing a minor theological offence so obscure as to have no name.

It was an unimportant Mass-of-the-day from the back of the book, a splendid catch-all designated "For A Holy Woman Neither Virgin Nor Martyr". The page I had abstracted carried only the second part of the heading, which therefore gave it a wider significance than the compiler had intended, and "neither virgin nor martyr" seemed to me a better commentary than Thoreau's generalisation about the majority of men. It was also a charming souvenir of the old God's day, when He still gave a damn, and Masses came under different titles but all the one flavour of varnished pine and dusty tiles, and all in a Giant Family Economy Size while trapped bees bumbled away the ritual hour behind cheap stained glass. I remembered a report of a Cultural Festival at an American college where, among lectures on Schoenberg and Arp and Mann, the Religious Department had presented a sequence of Masses in assorted flavours, like candy bars. You could take your pick from classics like the Missa Brevis of Couperin Le Grand, or with-it stuff like a Psychedelic Multi-Media Mass that had to take place in the Science Lab. Milton, thou shouldst be living at this hour. If the "scrannel pipes of wretched straw" so infuriated you, what would you have said about banjoes? They'd really have blown your mind.

I remember then the delicious speculations of some atomic researcher, struck by the proliferation of sub-atomic particles circulating in the vast empty spaces below the reach of a microscope, protons and neutrons and positrons and quirks and quarks, themselves merely packets of electricity in different flavour, shuffling in and out in their spheres of influence as they absorbed or shed quantas of juice. It was, he pointed out, a perfect mirror image of the larger universe. The world, the solar system, all the galaxies were, he insisted with the most heroically straight face, merely the inside of an atom which was part of a molecule which was part of the millions of cells that made up the left kneecap of God.

There was a minor commotion at my feet. I looked down and saw that two colonies of ants were battling furiously over the biscuit crumbs. One lot was lightly lighter-coloured and nimbler than the other, but the darker colony seemed to be more heavily armoured and that battle was evenly matched. The dust was littered with torn limbs and bisected bodies. Fianníocht stuff – *iomdha abach incinn agus ionathar ar chosaibh lán-láidre laoch.** Like God, I watched from on high and blessed both sides in their just war.

Two slender ants stood apart from all this, absorbed in higher things than the mere reflexes of hunger. One dark, one pale, one doubtless a Montague and the other a Capulet. Like the current pairings of the human young, I assumed in my old-fashioned way that they were of different sexes even if I could not tell which was which.

How charming! each was saying.

Nobody has ever really understood or appreciated me before. What grace! What beauty! What courage! What a miraculous sense of humour! Where have you been all my life? Nothing like this has happened to me before. Nothing like this has ever happened to anyone before, or will again.

* *Brains and entrails scattered at the mighy hero's feet.*

At which point I reached for my cheap tin cigarette case and fumbled it and it fell on the young lovers and pulped them. I imagine that the thought of being wiped out by God's cigarette case might have pleased them: at least it added a new twist to the old story.

I salvaged my case and wiped the tiny dusty mess from it, lit a cigarette and then noticed yet another unembattled ant, a scruffy grey fellow who scrabbled by himself in the dust. I looked over his shoulder and saw that he was trying to write words. "They had but looked out at the green fields", he wrote, and then went back and brushed furiously along the phrase, obviously realising that in this lion-coloured landscape green fields were meaningless. I could see him storing away the notion in his tiny little mind, and someone somewhere would one day babble of green fields.

Meanwhile he went and scrabbled again and amended the phrase to read "They had but looked up at the white clouds", and then he crept back to admire his work. I stood up in disgust and stood on him and put a stop to his nonsense. Secondhand Shakespeare would have been bad enough but, even though admittedly he was nearer to Rimini than to Verona; secondhand Stephen Phillips was intolerable.

I began to walk slowly back towards Bologna, keeping a hopeful eye out for Fred. There was a faint twinge in my knee, which half an hour earlier I would have dismissed as a sign of age. Now I preferred to think that in there, inside an atom, the whole story was being repeated, in whatever unimaginable terms were appropriate to its particular little universe. And so ad infinitum. We are neither virgin nor martyr but merely electric charges, divided into our two sexes of AC and DC. The world is not imminent in the mind of God. A whole infinite series of worlds is immanent in His left kneecap. And I hope it hurts.

THE HEROES

It was a sharp evening, with a touch of frost in the October air. Boys still loitered inside the gateway of the country school. A quartette played handball against the gable with a battered sponge ball, which bounded erratically from the peeling plaster, hopped crazily on the uneven earth of the playground, and sometimes went out of play entirely when it struck a corner of the name-board on which the faded letters MEENSHA N.S. could barely be distinguished.

The boys were talking of football, of the great deeds that had been done in their grandfathers' days, of the pre-historic band of heroes who had actually won the All-Ireland for the parish and for a less distinguished posterity. The trouble, said the fathers, was that the game had fallen on evil days. The micky-dazzling you saw these days wasn't football at all; all this hand-passing and fancy work was for trick-of-the-loop men and camogie players. Thus they clung to the old haphazard hallowed methods, and consoled themselves with 'sagas of ancient glory'.

"Any of yiz like to play a match tomorrow?" asked Joe Murphy.

"Yes!" answered a chorus of voices.

"Where?" asked the stragglers, the doubtful ones.

"Parkbeg," said Joe, "They have the lend of the Castle grounds for the day. They said they'd bate us home".

"They wouldn't bate butterflies," said big Jim Whelan

loudly. "For all they bate every other school in the barony. We'll skelp 'em".

"We will," agreed the voices.

"Two o'clock so," said Murphy, "let every last one of yiz be at the crossroads, for the honour of Meensha".

"But," said little Davy Ryan cautiously, "what about school? We're not all going mitching, are we?"

They turned and glared at him; he seemed to grow even smaller. Joe slowly stretched out finger and thumb, seized Davy's ear, and led him protesting through the gateway. He pointed to a wall beyond the road, where the remnants of a poster, held down by a large stone, flapped in the breeze. "Vote for Mulligan!" said the poster. It had also contained a string of promises; but the local humorists had scrawled in some slight alterations, to such good effect that the scandalised sacristan of the local church had torn away the rest of the poster, including the picture of the candidate. There were some who held that this improved Mulligan's chances, never very bright.

"See that?" said Joe.

"Yes," said Davy, wriggling.

"Well, when's the election?"

"To-morrow."

"And where's the voting?"

"In the school, of course. I forgot."

"Forgot," said Joe in horror, "forgot we'd the day off?" He twisted Davy's ear unmercifully. Davy yelled, kicked him in the shins, wriggled free and ran away, rubbing his ear. "Don't forget again," yelled Joe after him. "Two o'clock!"

The village public-house, by noon, contained seven customers, the daytime equivalent of a roaring trade. At two o'clock five more people had arrived, and the place was crowded. The benches along the wall were full, and men sat on the sloping lids of meal-bins. In solitary state on the single counterstool, the returning-officer consulted his watch and ordered a last drink. The customers circulated the latest joke about Mulligan audibly. The returning-officer, known to be a supporter of that lost cause, but gagged by his temporary trade, suffered visibly.

Outside, at the crossroads, the boys gathered by twos and threes, their nailed boots slung around their necks by knotted leather thongs. Joe Murphy, son of a strong farmer, had managed to secure a pony and trap on the pretext of ferrying his father's friends to the polling booths. Eight of the boys crowded into it. The pony jibbed in startled protest until the back of the trap banged into a wall.

Then there was a wild "Hurroo!" and a batter of hooves around the corner, and Whelan's jennet came galloping into sight, mallet-headed, long-maned, prancing, the flat cart leaping over potholes. Jim leaned back on the reins, and the jennet slid to a stop, almost on its haunches. The rest of the boys raised a cheer and scrambled on. They set off singing "Boolavogue" at the tops of their voices, up the narrow twisting road that led over the hills from the village.

The fields were muddy and pallid after a month of rain. Bare trees combed the horizon. Hawthorns, rotted to a purplish brown, dropped in the hedges. Only the holly and ivy held a splash of green. The lay-bys at the roadside held clumps of mud-coated sugar-beet, stacked ready for the lorries to collect. The boys piled off the carts and snatched handfuls of the beet, battered off the mud against the floorboards, and chewed great hunks of the sweet gritty pulp.

The road flattened out and the hedges grew higher. The village of Parkbeg came in sight, its cluster of houses staring at each other across a three-cornered green with a horse-trough, a chestnut tree and a broken bench. The boys turned off to the left before they came to the village, through a pair of huge stone gateposts and up a long dark drive where grass grew between the cart ruts. They came out from among tall clumps of box and privet and saw the parkland where cattle grazed among scattered trees, stretching away towards the Castle, a squat building with a tower at one end, whose ugliness was slightly disguised by the russet-coloured creeper which swarmed over it.

They skirted the park and made their way around to the playing field behind the Castle, where a wire fence enclosed the only reasonably level space for miles around. The Parkbeg team were there already, kicking a ball around. They had commandeered the little toolshed that served as a dressingroom. The Meensha boys tethered the pony and the jennet to a tree.

O'Donnell, the Parkbeg schoolmaster, came to meet them. He was a tall hearty man with a red face and hairy hands who was given to bursts of irrational rage, but thought himself a great favourite with the boys. His pupils capered about, and stuck out their tongues at him behind his back. The Meensha boys shuffled their feet and looked at the ground. Red Hugh was no favourite of theirs either. Why hadn't they been told he was coming? This wasn't fair.

"Well, well," said O'Donnell, rubbing his hands, "so we're all here! Fifteen. That's right. Well, don't let's stand around in the cold. Who's Captain ?"

"Me," said Joe Murphy, looking around truculently for any sign of disagreement. The others nodded.

"Well," said O'Donnell, "call for sides and may the best team win. I'm sure Parkbeg will never be beaten on their own home ground". He leered at his pupils who smirked back.

Hayden, the Parkbeg Captain, a tall slim fellow whose father owned the biggest shop in the district and who was always a bit too well-dressed, won the toss. He bent down and tied the laces of his shiny football boots ostentatiously. The Meensha boys trotted away to the other end of the field and draped their coats over the wire fence behind the goal line.

"Now men," said Joe Murphy, "death or glory. Lurry 'em up, but don't let O'Donnell spot yiz." They walked back to their position, stamping their feet.

O'Donnell threw in the ball. The half-way line became a melée of tussling figures, kicking, clawing, elbowing, foul following foul so swiftly that O'Donnell could not snatch a suitable opportunity for penalising the Meensha side. When the struggle ended there were three Parkbeg boys stretched in the mud, and the Meensha forwards were away down the field in a thundering squad, the ball at their feet. They ran through and over the Parkbeg backs. Shielded from O'Donnell's sight, Billy Wilson picked the ball off the ground in full flight and kicked, too straight. The Parkbeg goalkeeper jumped mightily, just got his fingers to the ball, and it went over the bar for a point. First blood to Meensha.

Hayden, the Parkbeg Captain, whispered to his men before the ball was kicked out. It went to a small, solidly-built boy on the right wing, who set off like lightning along the touchline, then turned inwards in a flash and kicked the ball right across the field to a waiting forward. The Meensha boys raced out, but he passed the ball over their heads, and the Parkbeg forwards sped towards the goal, passing the ball from one to the other so rapidly the Meensha boys were left floundering and cursing. Finally the ball lobbed across the goalmouth, over the head of the Meensha keeper, to where Hayden was waiting to tap it between the posts. O'Donnell doubled up, slapped his knee, and almost forgot to blow the whistle.

The rest of the half was a savage struggle, with little either way. Davy Ryan, skirmishing on the left wing, got away with the ball once, but was thrown over the sideline by his speedier opponent. A Parkbeg boy was caught in a Meensha rush and had to be replaced. He sat disconsolately at the side of the goal, huddled in coats and nursing his ankle. Jimmy O'Neill, thirty yards from a clear goal, was tripped so flagrantly that even O'Donnell had to award a free, which added a point to the Meensha score but left them still in arrears at halftime.

They sat, gasping and rubbing their bruises, along the foot of the wire fence. They chewed sugar-beet and planned their campaign. The whistle went at last. They stood up stiffly and marched to the wars again.

The evening was closing down. Fog blotted out the upper branches of leafless trees. The cold and damp cut through flesh and grated on the bone. But the Meensha boys let their teeth chatter and wasted no energy in running about. They refused to be lured out of the goalmouth. The battle turned into a siege.

Then, from a kickout, the Meensha team moved into action, heedless of kicks or trips. The ball went across, high in the air, to Davy on the wing. He glanced behind and saw two huge Parkbeg boys descending on him. He jumped, got his fist to the ball, tapped it over their heads and dodged around them. He went down the sideline, tipping the ball on his toe, until a half-back left his position and raced towards him. The charge caught him in mid-air and threw him, winded and sore all over, into a clump of thistles beyond the line; but his left-footed kick had sent the ball straight to Micky Wilson in the middle of the field. Micky dribbled the ball ahead, his brother Billy and Jimmy O'Neill running shoulder to shoulder with him. They trampled over the full back as if he were a cockroach, and ran straight through the goalkeeper and between the posts. Two points ahead, and ten minutes to go.

From the throw-in, Billy Wilson went away with the ball, but he was grabbed by the leg and tripped up under O'Donnell's nose. No whistle blew. The ball went away towards the Meensha goal. Joe Murphy, jumping, slipped on a muddy patch and went down. Hayden got the ball and awkwardly lobbed it high, in the general direction of the goal. A Parkbeg boy, with desperate bravery, leaped between two Meensha backs and fisted the ball blindly over his head. He picked himself up, scraping mud from his face, to see the football strike the inside of the upright, bounce on the crossbar, drop in the goalmouth, and, with its last vestige of spin, roll slowly across the line. A point behind once more, and five minutes to play.

"Sound lad," shouted O'Donnell, "Play up, Parkbeg!"

The kick-out was long and high. Billy Wilson was there, but two Parkbeg boys held on to his arms and the ball went safely past, to be fielded by the centre-field men, who passed it back to an unmarked man behind. Billy looked in expectation at O'Donnell, five yards away, but the teacher gave no sign of having seen the foul. Billy's face grew red. A Parkbeg boy came dodging through. Billy tackled him, and, hidden from O'Donnell, kicked him in the ankle. The boys yell was lost in the mud as Billy's knee landed in the middle of his back. "Blame O'Donnell," gasped Billy into his ear.

Billy straightened up with the ball at his feet. He saw O'Donnell ten yards away, and Micky Wilson twenty yards further off to his right. Between him and Micky two opponents were charging down on him. He steadied himself and kicked. The muddy ball struck O'Donnell behind the ear, hurling his cap in the mud, and ricocheted to Micky's feet. Micky ran up the field and passed to Davy. Davy dodged a half-back and passed back to Micky. They were in the centre of the field with only twenty yards to go. Ten yards to go. Five yards. Then the two small boys were lost under an avalanche of bodies. But the ball trickled clear, and Jimmy O'Neill, coming up fast, scrambled it past the goalkeeper.

The Meensha boys gathered around Davy and Micky as they whooped air into their straining lungs, shaking their hands and slapping them on the back while they stumbled down the field.

"It must be time up long ago," said Joe Murphy, "Where's O'Donnell?" They looked around.

"Gone home with a pain in his lug," said Hayden bitterly, "The score doesn't count if the referee isn't there. We won".

"Damn sure yiz didn't," said Joe cheerfully, "Ye were bet fair and square, and take yer batin' like men. But 'tis nothing to the batin' ye'll get from O'Donnell in the morning, to judge by the look on his ugly face the last I seen of him". The Meensha boys all laughed. Hayden took a step towards them, with his fists half-raised. Then he dropped his hands and turned away towards the shed. The other Parkbeg boys managed a feeble grin, and then followed him.

The bigger boys hoisted Micky and Davy onto their shoulders and moved towards the fence. A flight of rooks went harshly overhead. Then: 'Holy God!" said Jimmy

O'Neill, "Will yiz look at thim cows!" He screeched piercingly and ran forwards, waving his arms. The cows, which had been resting their necks contemplatively on the fence, tossed their heads in fright and lumbered off into the fog.

The boys picked up their coats in horror. All the pockets, filled with bits of sugar-beet, had been chewed away. Some had lost sleeves and collars as well. One boy was left with two strips of sodden cloth, no bigger than a baby's waistcoat. Fifteen scarecrows stared at one another with white faces. They looked wildly around the deserted field, with the fog closing in.

Music drifted from the castle as they skirted the park. A lantern bobbed among the trees where a workman was bringing in the cattle to be milked. A sheepdog barked. A door opened and let out a shaft of warm light across the gravelled space before the main entrance. Someone laughed.

The boys went down the drive, silently. Their tatters were no defence against the damp chill of the evening. The huddled together on Whelan's cart. They huddled together in Murphy's pony-trap. Every bruise and wrench began to ache. They turned out onto the main road and began to travel uneasily, homeward.

The road was barely visible, a lighter strip between the deeper darknesses of the hedges, but the pony and the jennet showed no hesitation. They strained into the traces and trotted up the long hill, eager for home and fodder.

At the top of the hill the pony broke into a canter and drew away from the boys in the cart. Jim Whelan raised his foot and kicked the jennet in the tail. The great mallet head jerked savagely upwards, the ears flattened back, the iron-shod hooves struck streams of sparks from the rocky road.

The cart slewed towards the ditch and the boys grabbed suddenly at one another. Then they were away down the narrow road at a gallop. Inside a hundred yards they caught the pony and trap. They scraped past, one wheel running up on the roadside bank and tilting the cart so that the boys nearly slid into the road. They held on, with their fingers wedged into cracks in the floorboards.

Jim Whelan was standing precariously with one foot on the shafts, yelling at the top of his voice and lashing the jennet to further effort. The wind whistled in their ears and froze their bones, and the cart leaped and jounced over the rough road. When the initial terror wore away, the exhilaration of the headlong rush through the darkness gripped them. They were yelling and cheering as they swung round by the public-house in Meensha and slid to a stop.

"What shouting have yiz, in God's name?"said the men, "Did yiz never get a holiday before?"

"The cows ate our coats," said Jim, "and we'll be skinned alive when we get home. But, be the powers of man, we bet Parkbeg!"

"Sure 'twas kind father for yiz," said the men. "Why wouldn't yiz indeed? There was never a team in Ireland could bate Meensha since the making of the world!"

And then the door closed and the singing started, and the conquering heroes scattered to their homes, their small figures seeming enlarged by the gathering mist until already they looked like giants in an old, old fable.

A SMALL GREEN HOLLOW LIKE A GRAVE

Something died that March day. Once upon a time death was a simple concept for most people, but recent squabblings about its clinical definition among the heart-snatchers have made us aware that it isn't perhaps so simple at all. Country-dwellers have known this all along, having watched on occasion a decapitated hen, staggering around a barnyard, aware only that it couldn't see but not that it was dead. It takes time to realise the fact of death, and meanwhile the body goes on going through the motions, defying mortality.

At intervals in the past ten years I've been poking around in that village in search of something indefinable. Last summer I seized the opportunity of showing it to a young American who wanted "to see some typical Ireland". She appeared to be paying flattering attention to everything I said, but it turned out later that she hadn't understood a single word of the dialect which is all I'll ever retain of that village now; possibly she thought I was speaking Gaelic instead of English. For her it may have been a typically quaint episode in a flying visit. For me it still represents a complex but soluble equation, the answer to which might explain me to myself. I'd overlooked a few important variables, including my own endurance and tenacity. It took me several weeks after that last trip in March to realise that it was the last trip, that I'd finally buried my childhood in that small green hollow with its secret intact.

My sister was a very quiet child; I suppose she would have been about four at the time; she had a round pale face, long dark ringlets, and big dark eyes, which looked very steadily at you, but without the curious, inquiring gaze of most children. She never laughed or cried; it satisfied her just to stand and watch, but it made the neighbours uneasy – they could never know what she was thinking. "A grand child, God bless her," they would say to my mother, "a grand child surely. It must be a great comfort to you not to have her shouting around the house like our own brood, God help 'em." And then they would bustle away down the lane, with their baskets on their arms, and my mother would smile strangely at us, and go into the house. But when my mother wasn't around, the neighbours said: "Those Casey children are unnatural, the Lord between us and all harm." I never had much to say for myself, either, and the two of us wandered around the country lanes on our own, with our hands clasped, and not talking at all – like twins, each of whom knows the other's mind, although there was a year between us. We lived happily in our own small world.

Somehow, it was always summer in those days, and the days were very long. There was sunlight always, and flowers along the grassy banks of the lanes.

Away beyond the hills, a mowing-machine would be working in Stacey's meadow, and the sleepy sound came clearly through the warm air. If you stood quietly in the shade of the hedge, the young rabbits came out along the headlands and frisked on the grass. Poppies burned in the meadows, and sometimes you found a skylark's nest hidden away in the grass, and could spend an hour looking at the tiny eggs in the little twist of dry yellow hay, lined with hair and fluff, while the mother bird trailed her wings along the ground a little space away. We had no consciousness of evil; it never occurred to us that anyone should wish to steal the eggs or damage the nest; the bird's antics interested us, so that we stood and watched, but we never sought to know their reason; we thought, perhaps, that it would be nice if she came closer, for why should she be afraid of us, who meant no harm?

Saturday afternoons were the best, for then everything seemed hushed by the quivering sun. A cart went down the lane, and you could hear each small, separate sound of its movement – the rumble of iron wheelbands, the scraping side-slip over a stone outcrop, the dull sound when the wheels ran over a muddy place on the road, the jingle of breeching and the squeak of harness, the tingling screech of a dry axle-block, and the monotonous sounds of hoofs on the cart-ruts; and sometimes the driver would be whistling to himself as he went down the dusty road to the village. We went through the yard gate, and followed the sound of the cart, trailing our feet in the floury dust and kicking it up in clouds around, our hands damply joined and a bird singing in the sun above.

A car came tearing along the road, almost grazing us where we walked by the hedge, and was gone around a bend with sudden blare on a horn, but we took no notice. The dust whirled and eddied, settling slowly on the leaves of the wayside bushes. We climbed down into the ditch, where wild strawberries grew under screens of furry leaves; they were scarce and small, but we were easily satisfied, and went on to the village with a few berries turning to a red smear in our small hands.

The street was deserted, except for the carpenter, who had a long baulk of timber propped against the front of his shed, and was trimming it for use as a cart-shaft; he looked small in the distance, but we could see the movement of the adze, and the flash of sunlight from the blade as it paused at the top of its swing, then the streak of light as it fell swiftly. A long time afterwards we heard the dull sound as it bit into the timber, and we stood there for a while, listening. Nothing else broke the stillness. The village dogs lay curled in the shadows, fast asleep.

On the corner of the crossroads, the door of the public-house stood open, and a bicycle leaned against the bars on the screened window. A mingled, heavy smell of porter, grain and tobacco came through the door, for Farrell's was also the village general dealers. We crept in unnoticed. Along the far wall were a row of tall bins, holding flour, bran, pollard and yellow meal, and the floor was scattered with sawdust over the uneven flagstones. A pair of copper scales hung from a pulley above the counter, and twists of tobacco stood on the back bar among bottles of whiskey; the shelves behind the counter held lemonade and glasses, and a cracked mirror with the face hidden by an advertisement. Auction posters covered the walls, and an advertisement for Duffy's circus made a bright splash of colour.

Sometimes Jimmy Farrell would give us the sheet of lead-foil from an empty tea-chest, if he was in a good humour. We stood there in the corner of the doorway, hidden by the shadow, as quiet as mice. Jimmy leant over the counter, reading a newspaper, and talking to a man who was drinking a pint.

"Powerful dance a Saturday night," said Jimmy, looking up from the paper, "yeh should have been there. I met the young one that lives beyond be the quarry."

"A bad wan, that," said the other man.

"Bad is it, ye say?" said Jimmy, laughing. "Be the hokey, d'yeh know – "

"Whist," said the man abruptly, "don't yeh see the childher there in the corner?"

Jimmy leaned over and strained his eyes into the shadow. "I wish to God them childher would make some noise so yeh's know they were in it. Gwan to hell outa that!" he roared suddenly. We could hear his voice complaining as we went out into the sunlight.

The midges were dancing over the little stream by the roadside. We tried to catch a glimpse of the big trout which was reputed to live under the flagstone where a path crossed the stream, but it must have been disturbed by the sound of our footsteps, and we saw only the eddy in the water, and the puff of sand kicked up by the speed of its rush to hiding. A guinea-fowl was screaming metallically in the farmyard beyond the high wall, and a ringing sound of metal came from the forge on the triangle between two roads. Little tufts of dry grass filled the spaces between the cobbles in the yard, and the ring- shaped stone for heating wheelbands was stained with marks of old fires. Bits of rusted iron and old horseshoes lay under a bush in the corner, together with a twisted bicycle wheel, and a broken ploughshare.

It was dark inside the forge; the fire was banked over, and only a tiny red glow came from it. Thin shafts of sunlight came through cracks in the slated roof, like bars of dusty steel. We stood in the doorway for a while, until our eyes became used to the dimness, and we could see where Paddy was working at the anvil, filing the cutters of a mowing-machine blade. He was a small man, with hunched shoulders and bandy legs; his eyes were always red from the smoke, and his hands twisted and covered with scars. He was said to be the strongest man in the five townlands that met at the village cross; the neighbours said that he could pick up the anvil – heavier than an ordinary man – with one hand, and that he had once pulled a beet-lorry out of a ditch, unaided. The knowledge of his own strength made him quiet, never joining in the arguments when the crowd gathered into the forge on rainy days. He took no notice of us standing in the door, but went on with his work, whistling through his teeth.

We stole in, and edged along the wall to the dark corner behind the bellows, where we sat on an old butter box. After a while he stood the blade against the wall by the door, and came back with a bar of iron, the end of which he pushed into the fire, then he began to work the bellows, and the forge filled with sound – the deep, sighing intake of air on the upstroke, the squeaking of leather and wooden bearings, the roar of the fire on the downstroke. The glow of the fire increased, and the flames began to leap from it, gradually lighting up the end of the forge, showing the smoke curling up along the blackened slope of the back wall, and vanishing through a hole in the roof.

In a few minutes, he took out the bar, which now shone whitely, and chopped off a length of it on the anvil. He took up a clumsy-looking pincers and a sledge-hammer, and began to manipulate the red-hot metal with expert speed, aiming it and pounding it from a flat strip into a rod of almost square section, by which time it had cooled, and was returned to the fire to be heated again. Then he began to bend it around the conical point of the anvil, until it reached its final shape, and turned up the ends with two swift blows;

finally he punched the holes for the nails – three on one side and four on the other. The finished horseshoe was now grey and covered with dull flakes; it looked cold, but when he quenched it in the stone trough, the water boiled furiously for a moment, sending up clouds of steam. He threw the shoe in a corner with a pile of others, and went to stand in the doorway. We found a shiny new nail, and began to trace designs in the dust of the floor.

We heard a loud, trampling sound on the cobbles in the yard. Paddy moved out into the light, and came back leading a huge grey horse, which limped badly on the offside rear hoof. The horse seemed to fill the forge completely, blotting out the light from the door, and we huddled closer into the corner out of sight. A young farmer came in and leaned against the work-bench: he looked worried.

"Must have picked up a stone, Paddy," he said, "I'm losing a day with the mowing, and the weather won't hold up long the way it's going." He came over and lit a Woodbine from the fire, and stood there dejectedly.

"Yeh could be worse off," said Paddy, "wait now till I have a look at this fellow." The horse stood quietly, with head hanging. Paddy stroked his hand down the horse's leg as far as the hock, then gently coaxed the hoof from the ground; the horse shivered and tossed its head.

"Aisy there, boy, aisy now," murmured Paddy. "The shoe is twisted at one side; yeh hit a rock, boy. Yer right about the stone, it looks bad enough."

He let the hoof drop, and searched among the heap of shoes until he found the biggest. Then he went to the bench and took a bone-handled knife and an iron spike. "Hold his head, John Joe," he said, "he's likely to kick." John Joe twisted one hand in the horse's mane, and began to stroke its nostrils with the other.

Paddy bent down, and rested the hoof, bottom up, on his leather apron. He straightened the ends of the old nails where they projected through the sides of the hoof, then ripped off the shoe, and began to pare the hoof. The horse jerked its hindquarters away from Paddy, who lost his grip on the hoof, and staggered to one side. John Joe was pushed backwards to the edge of the fireplace before he regained control, and he gave a sudden curse. Paddy spat on his hands, and gripped the hoof tightly between his legs; he began to dig at the stone in the frog of the hoof, which was surrounded by a raw patch.

Suddenly the horse lifted its head, tearing free from John Joe's grasp, and lunged backwards. Paddy stumbled, and the spike appeared to slip and bite into the centre of the hoof. The horse gave a high whinny of pain, which echoed in the small space, and then he slewed around, throwing Paddy violently out the door. Its battering hooves raised a cloud of dust from the concrete floor, and there was a crash of iron as it trod on the heap of shoes in the corner. Through the dust, we could see the pale form pitching and rearing between us and the light, and saw that the horse had turned completely around. It kicked out savagely with its hind legs just as John Joe leaped forward. There was a terrible, soft, tearing sound, and something splashed our faces as we cowered in the corner: then the horse galloped through the door, and crashed over the cobbles, and we heard Paddy's voice shouting after it in the distance; there was no other sound.

In the awful stillness we could see the body lying back over the anvil, the broken body without a face, and then we ran out into the sunlight, my sister's small damp hand clutched in mine. We ran along the dusty road towards home until we could run no more, then stumbled along with our breath tearing our lungs and our hearts pounding. And now she gave a frightened, lost scream and began to cry, and I was crying too, for we had instantly become aware of mortality, and the purposeless evil of the world.

FREEBOOTERS

Spring. The tops of the mountains were hidden in drifts of mist, and the clouds were low over the fields. The air was hot and damp, full of the shrieks of seagulls following the ploughman over the humpy ground. Chocolate-coloured soil hissed quietly, monotonously back from the gleaming ploughshare, covering the soft young grass. The man's shoulders were sagging under the strain of a long morning's work, watching the line of the furrow, the depth of the sole-plate, his fingers clenched on the damp wooden handles, the reins chafing his unprotected wrists. Behind him, the gulls and rooks pitched and squabbled over the newly turned earth.

The big grey horse strained over the top of the rise and turned out onto the headland; it stood there for a minute, head hanging, while threads of steam rose from its broad, heaving flanks. The man leaned on his elbows on the plough-handles, and looked down over the valley, at the ribbon of road winding off into a fold of the hills. Around the distant slope, a black speck moved into view, followed by another. For a moment, the farmer watched idly; then, as the specks grew larger, his eyes caught a flash of colour, and he straightened up, with a calloused palm pressed against the small of his back. He rubbed the sweat from his forehead and eyebrows with the back of an earthstained hand, and watched the road again; then he looked around to where his young son was squatting by the ragged hedge, peering into a rabbit burrow. "Johnny" he said, "run home and tell your mother the tinkers is coming. Tell her to watch the chickens." The boy ran off, stumbling across the broken ground, and the farmer stood motionless on the skyline, watching the lurching cavalcade in the valley.

Three carts were jingling and swaying in line over the uneven surface of the mountain road. Behind them trotted a band of decrepit, miserable horses. The carts were heaped with old sacks and baskets, over which sprawled the travelling people. Their clothes were dirty and torn, and their faces were swarthy, with high cheek-bones and black, curly hair. On the leading cart, a tall man was slouched, with one foot trailing loosely over the edge, and the other planted on the offside shaft. The reins were looped carelessly over his left hand, and he swayed to the movement of the cart over the scattered rocks and wheel tracks. He wore a tattered jacket and an old pair of flannel trousers; the toes of the foot on the shaft projected through a broken shoe. His shirt was collarless, and around his neck he wore a dirty handkerchief. On his head was a shapeless cap, black with grease, the brim pulled low over one eye. A scar ran from below his eye to the corner of his mouth, giving him an appearance of sardonic humour. He whistled softly through his teeth, and beat time on the floor of the cart with his free hand.

Behind him in the cart, his wife lay propped on one elbow, her head and shoulders wrapped in a black shawl. "Jamesy," she said, "are we near the village yet?"

"Soon enough, woman," he replied, "Can't ye rest aisy?" He raised his foot from the shaft and gave a brutal kick to the big, brown jennet; it started convulsively, and broke into a lumbering gallop; the lantern which hung beneath the axle began to jump about on the end of its chain. The grey-brown mongrel cur, running in the shelter of the cart, lengthened in its stride, and the procession banged and screeched its way down the stony road towards the distant houses.

The Angelus began to ring from the church above the village as the carts turned into the street. The fair was nearly over. The dull strokes of the bell hung on the damp air. Frieze-clad farmers removed their hats and blessed themselves. The sound of loud voices and arguments stopped for a minute, and there was only the bellow of cattle being driven home. All the shop windows were barricaded against the press of people and animals. The ploughshares and harrows, the boxes of eggs, the barrels of porter, the bicycles and scythe-handles which normally stood on the pavements outside the shops had not been put in position that morning. Groups of men in heavy overcoats and leggings stood around at the edge of the road, talking of politics and the price of cattle. Here and there, a bargain was still being struck. A squat man with bandy legs was running a rangy, bony mare up and down the road. The mare's head was high, and her nostrils flaring red, while her hoofs splashed through the deep mud and filth on the road. She pranced sideways like a crab, and the small man caressed her nostrils with a practised hand. Around and through the standing groups the children were chasing, waving ashplants at one another, with shrill laughter.

The tinkers pulled in their carts at the gable of the market house, and spread out through the crowd, selling their wares – tin cans of all shapes and kinds, paper flowers, cheap glass vases, and patriotic ballads. They walked gracefully, catlike, among the heavy countrymen, and their dark eyes were fierce and compelling. Old Patsy and his wife stood outside the open door of the public house; he took an ancient concertina from under his arm, and began to stagger through the notes of a ballad, while the cracked voice of his wife cut through the loud talk inside the house. At the end of the song, they marched inside and began to sell their broadsheets of the ballad. The farmers were in good humour and bought freely and generously. When the last broadsheet had been sold, the publican called to the tinkers and set two pints of porter in front of them. It had been a good fair. The tinkers picked up the glasses and made their way to the back wall, where they stood in silence, drinking slowly. Their eyes were veiled and scornful.

Down by the market house, the dogs of the village had gathered in a half-circle around the carts, and were snarling at the strange mongrel. The grey, bedraggled dog sat in the mud under the cart, paying no attention to the others as long as they kept their distance. A dirty sheep-dog, bolder than the rest, sidled in from the group, and began to snarl softly. The mongrel came to its feet, with yellow eyes blazing. Its head was low, and the great ridges of muscle on its shoulders were quivering with power. The wet hairs on its back stood up in spikes, and a deep menacing rumble came from its throat; its paws were digging into the mud. The sheepdog slowly backed away, with its tail between its legs. Then Jamesy and his wife came around the corner and broke up the circle of dogs with kicks and loud oaths. The grey mongrel curled up again under the axle-tree.

Up on the hill-farm, a great cauldron of boiled potatoes stood in the centre of the flagged kitchen, and a middle-aged woman pounded them steadily with a broomstick. Outside, in the sty at the gable wall, the pigs heard the noise, and squealed impatiently for their food. An old tinker woman walked over the packed earth of the yard, and the chickens scattered before her. She stood in the doorway, holding a bundle of vases and other gew-gaws in the fold of her shawl. The woman inside looked up from her work, and shook her head with dull patience.

"No," she muttered, "nothing today".

"Any old coats or trousers for the childher?" asked the tinker, arrogantly. There was no reply. She stayed in the doorway, looking at the dim interior, the huge fireplace and battered deal table, the rough chairs, religious pictures and an old oil-lamp on the walls, a dresser laden with crockery, chicken-feathers and dust on the stone flags. Mag Carthy came around the western gable, by the bed of flagrant purple peonies; she was young, with a sultry, handsome face under a gaudy shawl, a figure like the curl of a whiplash, strength and grace in her movements. She looked at the old woman, who shook her head slightly. They gathered their shawls about them and went down the dusty road, leaving the gate swinging open behind them. Mag Carthy walked smoothly, feeling the weight of the stolen clutch of eggs in the curve of her arm.

The tinkers drifted back in ones and twos from their foraging, and the carts moved off towards the sunset. About a mile from the village they came to a grove of trees in a bend of the roadway. There was a broad grassy patch between the plantation and the road, and bushes flanked the clearing on either side. In the centre, the bare earth showed traces of old camp fires. They pulled in their carts on the grass in a circle, unharnessed the horses and tethered them among the trees. The carts were tilted up around the edge of the clearing, forming crude shelters; under them the old sacks and blankets were piled on the grass. The women brought dry leaves, twigs, and dead branches from the wood, and began to light a fire. Steam rose from the damp earth and the clothes of the tinkers. It was nearly dark.

Beyond the plantation was a meadow, fenced with briars and nettles, and beyond that again was a field of young wheat, the green shoots beginning to feather. Along the edge of the wheat-field, alders and willows grew in a dense screen, and behind them was the river. Trout lurked in the dark holes under the tree-roots, and an otter was crouched on a sand-bank by the tail of the deep pool. The moon was coming up, huge and red through the clearing mist, behind the black range of distant hills. It rose slowly, and as it passed above the belt of mist, it grew small and silver. Farther down the stream, the water gurgled over a shoal of broken rocks, and shimmered in the moonlight. Rain clouds were blowing up from the mountain, and began to blanket the sky; the moon hid in a black scarf of cloud, and the shallows were dark again. Closer to the bank, there was a deep channel, where the water ran with quiet power. Under the deeper shadow of a furze bush, a man lay like a corpse, curled up on his left side. In his right hand he held a crude three-pronged spear. Deep in the water he caught a flash of silver edging its way upstream. The muscles of his arm tensed, and the veins crawled in the back of his swarthy hand. He muttered an oath.

The water-bailiff, walking softly down the bank, heard the faint sound, and stepped behind a tree; he peered into the gloom, but could see no movement. A black shadow moved catlike behind him, and a hand closed over his mouth before he could cry out; he felt his hat crushed in under the weight of a heavy stone, muffling the impact, and he collapsed unconscious against the tree-trunk. The tinker looked down at the bailiff, and sneered. There was a flurry of sound from the furze bush, as Patsy jabbed the spear into the dark water, impaling the salmon. He rolled over on his back, and clutched the spear with both hands. It took all his strength to hold the handle against the agonized struggles of the twelve-pound fish, a first-run springer, fresh from the sea. After a minute of splashing and struggling, he catapulted the salmon out of the water, over the bush, onto the grass. His hobnailed boot descended with a crunch on the head of the fish; an electric shudder ran through the yard of molten silver, its gills opened convulsively, and then it lay still in the damp grass. He slipped his hand through the gills, slung the fish over his shoulder, and set off across the field, trampling the young green wheat.

The branches of resinous pine in the fire were beginning to splutter and crackle, sending out little jets of green and blue flame. The earth in a circle around the fire had been dried out by the heat, and the dancing flames reddened the under-surface of the leaves on the surrounding trees. The blue smoke curled up and away into the darkness over the road. A saucepan was bubbling against the side of the burning branches, and a brace of chickens turned on an impoverished spit over the flames. Some farmer's wife at that moment was dreaming of what she would do with the price of those chickens when they were ready for the market. She thought of the prowling fox, and stirred uneasily in her sleep.

The tinkers crouched on sacks around the fire, and ate greedily, ravenously, until the last morsel had been devoured, the frying pan scoured with the heel of a loaf of bread, and the three-legged skillet turned upside down to drain. They sat back, and produced short blackened clay pipes, which they filled with coarse black tobacco, cut from a twist like a root of gnarled bog oak. Glowing embers were pulled from the fire to light the pipes, and the tobacco-smoke drifted upwards, mingled with the smoke of the fire. Old Michael, the head of the clan, rose from his position, and rummaged in the heap of rags under his cart; he produced a large square bottle and came back to the circle of people squatting motionless on the ground. The clear liquid in the bottle sparkled like diamonds and rubies in the light of the flames. He wrenched out the cork with his strong, tobacco-stained teeth. The biting smell of the raw spirit filled the air. He tilted back his head and swallowed a good share of the potheen; the firelight picked out the straggling grey beard on his chin, and the broad flare of his nostrils. The bottle went around the group in silence, each one drinking and passing it to the next.

Then Jamesy laughed, a full-throated, deep chuckle. Patsy began, very softly, to finger the keys of the concertina, in an ancient tune, and Mag took up the song, singing quietly to herself. The red light of the fire, slanting upwards, caught the high swarthy cheekbones of the people around it, leaving their eyes in shadow. They sat there, as motionless as the trees behind them, feeling the warmth of the fire, and the food and drink inside them. Their faces were content and happy.

Beyond the road, beyond the farthest glow of the fire, the ground rose sharply to a rocky ridge, matted with heather and bracken. Stark in silhouette against the starry sky crouched the grey mongrel, while with upthrown head and full throat he howled at the full moon. Far away, in the next valley, by the sleeping farmhouse, the watchdog heard the call, where she lay in the corner by the rainbarrel. She came to her feet, and waited until the call came again, then slipped through the fence like a shadow, and began to lope across the field. Behind her, the farmer and his family slept soundly under the thatched eaves; in the outhouses, the fowl roosted quietly, while the fox moved softly on his belly through the weeds towards the low-lying buildings.

VLADIVOSTOK

[i]

May always promises summer, though June too often is a jilty jade. *For* (as has been written by Sir Thomas Malory, Knight, in older days) *like as herbs and trees bring forth fruit and flourish in May, in likewise every lusty heart, that is in any manner a lover, springeth and flourisheth in lusty deeds... Therefore all ye that be lovers call unto your remembrance the month of May, like as did queen Guenever.* For her, also, as did that ungentle knight, we make here a little mention, that while she lived she was a true lover, and therefore had she a good end: not that the deduction follows.

[ii]

It was a day in May with a crisp breeze and a cold, turbulent sea. Joe Walsh trotted briskly up the beach, swinging his arms vigorously across his chest and nodding his head to shake the water out of his ears. Across the wet sand, across a fringe of seaweed, across dry powdery sand, to the shingle at the foot of the sea wall that edged the promenade, where his clothes were heaped under an old raincoat. He bent down to drag his shirt from the tangle of clothes.

"Well, Tarzan," said a voice overhead, "how was it?"

Joe looked up, startled, at the girl sitting on the wall, belted into a heavy coat. How long had she been there? She had a curiously small, white face, spotted with dark freckles, and topped by an untidy mop of jet-black hair, the colour, and apparently the consistency, of tarred barbed wire. A wicked little smile twisted a mouth on which too-light lipstick was smeared a shade too widely. Joe's nineteen years had not given him much practice in dealing with girls, especially girls who wore wicked little smiles and too-light lipstick. He stood speechless with the shirt trailing at his side.

"Well?" she asked again, and the smile broadened.

"Oh," he said, "grand. Grand. At least it's grand when you're in. But if you're going swimming, watch out for the undertow. It's a holy terror to-day."

"Me?" she said, in horror. "Is it me get into that water? Do you think I've no more sense than yourself?"

Joe was suddenly conscious that he was blushing all over. He struggled damply into his shirt, emerging, breathless and clammy, with his hair standing up in spikes. He slipped out of his trunks, wriggled into his trousers, flattened his hair onto his skull with the palms of both hands, and jammed his feet into his already laced shoes. He slammed the wet trunks against his shin to rid them of sand, stuffed them into one pocket of the raincoat and threw the coat over his arm. He was dressed and ready to go home.

"Well, my God," said the girl, "but you're hardy characters around this terrible place. Don't you ever catch cold?"

"No," said Joe, shuffling his feet in the shingle as though he had dropped a coin and was looking for it, "Why should we? Nothing healthier than seawater."

He took a last look around the strand, then began to scramble up the steep slope of the wall. She reached over and grabbed his wrist as he came near the top, and heaved with surprising strength. He leaped over onto the promenade, and it seemed that her hand lingered on his wrist for a brief moment longer than was absolutely necessary.

"Funny time for holidays," said Joe, "I suppose you are on holidays? I know every sinner in this town and I've never seen you before."

"I suppose so," she said, looking round at the deserted promenade, the empty strand, the closed houses with unweeded gardens. "Cheerful little graveyard you've got here. I saw a date over a doorway in the town. Fourteen hundred and something. Funny thing: it was the newest-looking house in the street. What is there to do around here?"

"Oh," said Joe, "there's a dance twice a week at the Pavilion, and the Technical students have a play at the Town Hall. And then, there's the pictures, of course."

"That's right." she said, "the pictures. A revival of Ben Hur, and a Western I saw four times already. And three days before the next dance. A mad whirl of pleasure. What wouldn't I give for a good swing band right now!" Her toes tapped out a rhythm on the concrete.

A gust of wind blew sharp sand and scraps of paper against their faces. They turned, huddling into coat-collars, to face out along the long curve of yellow strand that reached for miles towards a hazy headland. In all those miles nothing stirred, except little sand-devils twirling in the breeze.

"What do you do to kill the time?" she asked.

'I never thought about it much," said Joe, "I suppose I just let it live." He laughed suddenly. "I swim a lot, from April to November. Once I kept it up right through the year, but it gets a bit dangerous in winter. See those rocks there?" She followed the line of his pointing finger. She saw a line of great jagged rocks standing some distance away from the foot of the sea-wall. "That's the remains of the old wall," he said. "Some of those rocks weighed half a ton. It only took one good storm and ..." He clicked his fingers expressively.

"I see," she said shivering.

"I play a lot of billiards in the winter. And, of course, I fish most of the time."

"Fish..." she said. She stood up. "Well... The only good thing I see about this place is that I'll only be seeing it for one day more. We had a bit of an accident at the factory – refrigerating plant blew up. Hell of an explosion and the whole place swamped with ammonia fumes. Some of the girls are in hospital with gas-poisoning and shock, and the plant's out of action anyway, so the boss very kindly gave us a few days off. Bet the old so-and-so will try to take it out of our summer holidays. And I got a mad notion to come down here because I'd heard so much about it! God help us all. I'd have been better off in the hospital."

"Ah, now," said Joe, "it isn't fair to judge it by to-day. On a Bank Holiday week-end you couldn't cross the road there for the press of cars, and you couldn't see a square foot of strand for people. Every house open and lighted up, and wirelesses playing. The two dance-halls going full-blast, and a fun-fair down there by the railway station, and coloured lights all over the place. The crowd in the station-yard waiting for the last train home, and dancing half the night to melodeon music. Every pub in the town with its door bulging, and people with red raw sunburn eating ice-cream at midnight. Not that I'd enjoy it much, mind you, but the visitors seem to. Give me the autumn any time."

"You can have the autumn," she said sadly, "if you'll give me the Bank Holiday. Now I have to go home to dinner. I'm going to get my money's worth if it kills me."

"Where are you staying, by the way?" asked Joe. "I didn't think any of the hotels were open yet."

"They aren't really. See that place across on the back road?"

She pointed away across the marsh and the railway line, away to a squat building with ugly iron verandas and a purple-slated roof. "That's the joint. They said first they weren't open yet, but then I think their greed got the better of them. But I suppose when they came to their senses they realized they'd be losing money by opening the place for one customer, and they're certainly letting me know it. Guest of honour, that's me." She looked at her watch. "Oh God, I'll be late for dinner, and all they want is the excuse."

"No, you won't" said Joe. "You've got ten minutes, and there's a short-cut across the marsh, though you'd never get over it by yourself without getting stuck in the mud. Here, follow me."

He led the way across the road, along a narrow laneway between two houses, through a gap in a fence, and down an embankment on to open swampy ground tufted with tall rushes. She followed him cautiously, stumbling occasionally and swearing softly.

"Damn peep-toe shoes, anyway," she said, "every grain of sand and every drop of wet goes in and never comes out again."

"Now watch it," he said, 'and only step where I've stepped before you. Otherwise you'll be up to your neck in it." He began to zigzag slowly towards the railway-line, following the remnants of a causeway whose stones had sunk below the surface of the mud but left a mossy and slightly firmer footing. They stopped at the tracks to let a goods-train go slowly by; a cloud of smoke came chokingly down on them and drifted off over the marsh. They crossed the line, she staggering painfully on the sharp-edged ballast between the sleepers.

"Now," he said, "this is the worst bit, because there isn't any path, but if you grab the tail of my coat you'll be all right." She did so, without a word, and they went on, hopping warily from one clump of weeds to the next. Once she gave a muffled gasp, and once she tugged so hard at his coat that he nearly overbalanced. At last they came to the edge of the road.

He vaulted the stone stile and turned to give her a hand. She stood on top of the low wall, shoes muddy, cheeks red, black hair straggling over her forehead and a broad grin on her face. She was triumphantly waving a yard-long, sword-shaped leaf, with black mud clinging to its roots.

"Well," she said, "we made it."

"We did," said Joe. "Where did you pick up the felestrum?"

"Felestrum?" she said inquiringly.

"That thing," he said, pointing. "The flagger. Wild iris, I think, is the right name."

"Oh, she said, "so that's what they're called. I pulled it out of the swamp, the time I nearly pulled you off your feet. I thought It'd be a shame to die without having some souvenir of a lovely holiday." She wrinkled her nose at him and waved the flagger about her head. "Well, well. Wild iris. Wild iris: that's me – I grow wild in the bushes."

She brandished the green sword again and jumped down suddenly from the wall. Automatically, he caught her, and staggered a few paces onto the road; she was unexpectedly heavy. He stood there, holding her foolishly, until she pushed herself gently away.

"Dinner-time," she said. "The name's Iris, in case you hadn't guessed."

"Mine's Joe," he said. "Good luck for now," and walked away, confused. He turned once, and saw her standing still by the side the road, the wild iris trailing by her side. He waved. She waved; the green blade had been bent and flapped like a broken wing. Then he went on towards home.

[iii]

The old town drowsed content in the mildness of the afternoon, the morning's sharp breeze transformed to a gentle drift of air. The stretch of dun-coloured mud left between the dock walls by a falling tide shimmered with mirrored sunlight. Small boats sprawled athwart the mud, and tiny green crabs scuttled about in the shadow of leaning gunwales. Deep black caverns in the smooth mud showed where Joe had spent a couple of hours' furious activity digging lug-warms. He came slowly up the slipway, in one hand a heavy shovel, in the other a bucket half-full of the lumpy, bristly, liver-coloured creatures. There were splashes of mud on his face and a rent in the knee of his trousers.

"Yoo-hoo," said a light voice. He looked up and saw Iris coming down the street, kicking her heels on the pavement like a little girl playing hopscotch. He waited until she came nearer.

"Well, the hard-working man. So we meet again. What have you got in the bucket?"

"Worms," he said. "See".

She peered cautiously into the bucket, then clutched at

her throat. "Ugh, they're disgusting. Take them away. What are you going to do – eat them?"

"Good God, no! said Joe. "I'll use them for bait, of course. Maybe catch a few sand-dabs, or even a bass."

"I've never seen anything so horrible," she said. "When you said worms I thought you meant the little pink earthworms. They're bad enough, the wriggly things, but these – I'll have nightmares for a week."

Maybe I should tell her they've got greeny-yellow blood, thought Joe, gloating a little: that'd finish her completely. They stood there at the side of the dock, looking at one another warily.

"Well," she said, "what are you going to do for the rest of the evening? Dig up more worms?"

"No," said Joe. "I'm going up the embankment as far as the bridge to look for pill-crabs."

"Mind if I come too? I'm rightly fed up with myself."

"Sure," he said. "It's a nice walk on a fine evening." He laid the bucket of worms beside the wall and propped the blade of the shovel over the top of it.

"Will it be safe there? she asked.

"Of course," he said, surprised. "Who'd be bothered stealing it in this place? We're terrible honest here – in small things, anyway."

They went laughing along the wide, dusty, deserted street where dogs slept on the pavement. They walked in the shadow of a tall warehouse whose walls were crumbling, whose windows were blocked with sheets of rusty corrugated iron. They passed the market-house in a cobbled square where a laneway came in under a Norman watergate, and came out on the fair green, a wide uneven space of sparse grass and tall thistles, with a great rusty anchor lying in the middle of it like a stranded whale. To their left, seagulls and crows squabbled over a dump. Farther out, a gannet dropped, spearing slantwise from high air into the slacktide estuary. There was no other sign of life or movement.

They climbed a gentle slope to the top of the embankment. On one side weed-covered boulders dropped steeply away to where grey scummy water sucked and gurgled. On the other side a grassy incline went down to a salt meadow, rank with brown weeds, where a few cows grazed forlornly in the distance. A long, narrow, muddy point ran parallel with the embankment, its steely surface jagged with tiny ripples.

The breeze frolicked around them as they stood unsheltered, gazing at the wide and featureless prospect. Off on their left stretched the estuary, current curling serpent-like across its leaden surface, a trail of yellow swirling foam marking the dividing-line between the slate-blue-sea water and the muddy river channel. A salmon jumped far out on the edge of slack water. A cormorant bobbed along, sleek black head nodding, in the channel. The breeze carried a sour smell of mud and weed. Iris pushed out her chin and shook her hair out of her eyes.

"Oh," she said softly, "this is nice."

Joe looked at her, astonished. Then he looked back at the familiar scenery, trying to visualize it through unfamiliar eyes. It still looked the same. "Come on," he said at last, "let's go to the bridge."

She skipped ahead, leaping nimbly over the broken places where burdocks grew among the tumbled stones. They came to where a barbed-wire fence ran from the edge of the pond, up along the bank and across the path, rudely barring their way. She looked inland over the brown-olive herbage of the salt-meadow.

"How deep is the pond?" she asked. "Is there anything in it?"

"Yes," said Joe, "about three or four feet of water, but there's a few deep holes in it. We used to swim there when we were kids, but there are thousands of springs coming up through the mud and everywhere there's a spring there's a quicksand, so when we got sense we gave it up. See there?"

"Where?"

"In a line between us and that little bush on the far side. See that rough patch on the surface?"

"Oh, Yes. Yes, I see it now. What's so special about it?"

"That's a school of mullet. The place is full of them. Cutest fish in the sea. You can't catch them. If you try to net them, they jump the net. You can use two nets, one behind the other, and take them by surprise, but it takes a lot of boats, and who's going to bother?"

"Why not?"

"To tell you the God's truth," said Joe, "they taste like wet flannel. But I wish you could see some baby mullet. They're little silver things about as long as your thumbnail – perfect little fish, all the same – and they swim in perfect formation in little squads of five or six, spread out across a patch the size of your hand, and their little tails are buzzing so fast you can barely see them, and they're all swimming like the devil and getting no place much. You'd like them. But you're a couple of months too early." He stopped, embarrassed by his own enthusiasm and by the slight grin on her face.

"Yes," she said, "and I've to go home to-morrow morning. Think it'd be worth my while coming back – for the baby mullet?" There was something in the sideways tilt of her black head that suddenly reminded him of a sleek, dark cormorant speculatively eyeing a sprat, ready to pounce.

He grabbed the fence-post that leaned out over the seaward side of the embankment and swung nimbly around it, then with foot and hand opened a gap between the strands of wire wide enough for her to scramble through. He felt like shaking her. Her shoulder brushed against him as she straightened up, and the wire twanged suddenly from his fingers in abrupt resolution. But she was already some yards away along the bank.

[iv]

He walked a few paces and stopped, looking meditatively at a great thatch of olive-coloured weed on the rocks below. "Hey!" he shouted to Iris, "wait a minute for me." He scrambled down the embankment towards the grey, heaving water.

She turned, paused and slowly strolled back, hands in pockets, head bowed. "Well, little man," she said, "what now?"

"Pill-crabs," he said, looking up from his scrabbling among the weeds and in the crevices of rocks. "Remember I told you?"

"I must see this," she said excitedly. He looked up, started at the sound of her heels slipping on smooth water-worn rocks, and looked away, blushing. She recovered her balance, casually smoothed down her skirt, and came to stand beside him among the weeds, heedless of the oily moisture that soaked her shoes.

He grabbed at a hank of slippery bladder-wrack and pulled it away, together with the fist-sized rock to which its roots were fastened. In the puddle of dark water that filled the cavity, something scurried about. He plunged in his hand and brought out a pair of crabs – a big dark crab with great claws, one of which tightly enfolded a smaller, yellow-green crab whose claws were curled to rest. He threw away the bigger crab and turned with the other in his hand.

"See," he said, "there's a pill-crab for you." He twisted one of the crab's sharp walking legs. It cracked and pulled away like a torn sleeve; beneath, like an optical illusion, remained a soft, limp, yellow-green replica of the shell, perfect in every detail even to the minute dark serrations at the tip of the claw. "It's the same all over, the new shell grown under the old one that will be cast in a few days' time. And then, for the few days the shell is hardening, the crab is completely helpless – can't even move about. It's about as lively as a poached egg. That's why it goes away and hides in a crack of the rock. They're the best bait in the world for bass."

"But what about the other crab?" asked Iris. "The big one? Was it protecting the small one?"

"I doubt it," said Joe. "I'll bet it's only waiting for the small one to cast its shell so that it can eat it."

"Good God," said Iris. "That's disgusting."

He hardly heard her above the noise he was making, tearing away great clumps of seaweed and rolling rocks aside. He had taken a tightly-rolled small sack from his pocket, dipped it into the water and laid it among the weeds. As he came upon a crab he popped it into the sack. At last he hefted the sack, satisfied. "That should do," he said, straightening up.

She started up the bank, wincing now as her feet squelched in the weed.

"Mind," he warned. "That stuff's shocking slippery."

She grinned over her shoulder and went sure-footedly on. He began to follow, stepped on a loose stone which twisted side-ways beneath him, fell on his back and skidded down the weedy slope until he was up to his knees in sea-water. She gave a small scream, then, as he sat up shaking his head, she collapsed on the edge of the embankment and began to bellow with laughter.

He scrambled up the rocks, carrying the bag from which streamlets of water dripped on his sodden trousers. She was rocking from side to side, her arms clutching her sides and her hair swinging over the face. In a moment he began to laugh also. He grabbed her arm and pulled her to her feet and they clung together on the path until the fit of laughter passed and then they went on, arm in arm, towards the bridge.

The path widened out into a level space the size of a tennis court, covered with pebbles and tufts of dry grass, where the bridge, the roadway and the embankment met. They walked along the smooth tanked surface of the bridge until they came to the swinging middle-section, floored with uneven wooden blocks.

They leaned over the iron parapet, gazing down at the weed- fringed wooden piers that looked like deserted barges, at the deep channel surging and gurgling between the piers and fanning away downstream in a line of small whirlpools. Gulls – black, brown-backed and snowy white – bobbed on the wavelets or fluttered suddenly into the air. Staring at the smoothly rushing water, one felt the ridge to be slowly toppling backwards. It was a relief to look up and away to the mouth of the estuary and the two hills that guarded it.

One side of the estuary was a wide stretch of muddy slobland and a coast road which turned out of sight along a valley where a little stream came down to meander through the mud-flats. On the other side was the long line of the embankment by which they had come. Headlands came round to hold the harbour in an arm-grasp, one bare, rocky, scattered with small plantations of pine-trees, the other straggled with the houses of the small town and a lighthouse perched small and white against the sky.

Upstream, a little river came in under a low twin-arched stone bridge. Cattle stood knee-deep in its shallow waters. A heron rose from its one-legged stance near the bank and flapped clumsily away, like a tablecloth blown from a clothes-line by a sudden storm. The angle between the tributary and the main stream was filled by a promontory shaggy with pines, over which pylons strode away into the distance. Around and behind the promontory the foam-flecked river went twisting out of sight. The breeze sighed softly overhead, and squabbling seagulls sounded like rusty hacksaws.

Iris leaned back, her elbows resting on the parapet, and looked up the river. "It's wonderful," she said, and drew a deep breath. "I remember seeing a travel-film once about the Rhine. It looked just the same."

'That's what they tell me," said Joe. "It keeps twisting about for the next twenty miles, and woods all the way. If you go up in a boat you have to keep switching from side to side to keep out of the current, and sometimes you get so close to the bank you could nearly touch it, and the leaves hang down and almost brush against your face. And there are little cliffs where there always seems to be a goat looking down at you. It's nice all right. In the summer the Corporation runs trips up the river in motor-boats a couple of times a week. You'd like that. But you're too early in the year for it."

"Yeah," she said sourly, "too early. Everything's either too early or too late in this damn town." She picked up a pebble and hurled it savagely into the river. "'Why does nothing ever happen now? I haven't got all my life to wait. Why doesn't someone get some action around here?" She looked at him, and her mouth was a pale straight line. The bag of crabs dripped audibly against his shins.

The silence was broken by the sound of a labouring engine. An old lorry came creaking over the bridge and pulled groaningly to a stop. The driver stuck his head through the empty window-frame and wiped the perspiration from his face with the back of a floury hand.

"Hey, Joe," he shouted across, "what time is it?"

"Divil a know I know, Steve," said Joe. Hardly had he spoken than the sound of bells came softly across the water.

"There's the Angelus," he said. "I didn't think it was that late."

"Oh Lord," said Iris, "my watch must have stopped!"

"Do you want a lift into town?" asked Steve.

"Yes," said Iris, "but certainly. It'll save me from starvation."

She ran across and got in beside the driver.

"How about you, Joe?" he asked. "You'll have to get on the back."

"Good enough," said Joe, "provided her ladyship has the comfort." He vaulted up on to the flat floor of the lorry and sat on a pile of dusty sacks, his back to the wall of the cab and the sack of crabs heaving and wriggling beside him. The lorry began, shudderingly, to move. Everything in the back bounced madly at the slightest unevenness in the road. He could hardly hear their voices over the roar of the engine, but they seemed in merry humour. Trust Steve, he thought, with mingled annoyance and amusement. He heard Iris's voice raised in song. He caught a fragment of the meandering ballad.

Blackpool girls are fine and tall,
Up again' de Sunbeam wall.
Here's-

The noise of the engine blotted out the song. "The Boys of Fair Hill", he thought: they'd give you some action fast enough. I'm a fine hero, he thought, myself and my sack of pill-crabs. Then the lorry leaped and bounced over the pot-holes that mark the entrance to every small seaside town, and he grabbed at the sack just in time to stop it from sliding into the road. Inside the wet canvas the crabs bubbled and scrabbled indignantly as if to show that they still survived.

They passed under an old sandstone archway that straddled the main street, and the echo of the engine roared deafeningly down at them. They pulled up where a narrow side-street went down between leaning houses towards the harbour. Steve stuck his head around the side of the cab.

"This do you, Joe?" he asked.

"Sure," said Joe, hopping down to the path. "Safe home. See you on Saturday."

Iris looked out the window and waved casually as the lorry moved away. Joe stood there for a moment, then turned away down the side-street. I wonder, he said to himself, how she'll like it when she finds that Steve lives twenty miles farther on? Poor girl, you'll have a lonely last evening after all. He laughed, a little unevenly, and swung the dripping sack of doomed crabs.

[V]

Evening came clear and breathless. A wisp of fog trailed over glassy sea and made a brownish band against the lemon-coloured sky on the horizon. Swallows flew far above. The light lingered, but a dim, blue haziness blurred the outlines of the old warehouses, the crumbling archway, the boats riding at anchor in slack water. Inside the ugly building that housed the social club, shadows gathered. Joe wandered restlessly around the deserted billiard-room, reluctant to switch on the light and acknowledge another day's end. Sheeted billiard-tables loomed shapeless in the gloom.

He switched on the wireless and switched it off again before it uttered more than a crackle of static. He picked up a magazine and carried it to the window, twisting it in an attempt to catch the fading light, but the print swam before his eyes and he threw the magazine on a seat. He walked to the empty fireplace and stared at the dim, dusty trophies in their glass-case, its green baize faded to a streaky olive. He tapped his foot on the fender and listened to the dull ringing sound. There was nothing to hold his roving mind.

He began to whistle softy, until the tune turned into "The Boys of Fair Hill" and died away. He walked to the door, then, with his hand already on the light-switch, he paused for a moment, irresolute. The clock ticked away loudly in the stillness, then groaned and wheezed and struck nine. The sound sank into the shadows. Joe pulled open the door abruptly and went down the steps, to cool evening air and gravel that crunched underfoot.

A star glimmered in the east and night lurked, waiting, in corners. On the empty promenade a sea-breeze came, salt and weedy. Waves hushed and whispered far down the strand. On top of the cliff the air had a tang of blooming furze. Strange colourings wavered over the flat marshy land below, where the railway-line ran off out of sight and the green jewel of a distant signal was the only point of focus in a featureless landscape. Distance and size were alike deceptive. The factory on the upper road seemed no bigger than a matchbox, while small bushes were immense vague presences.

He walked silently along the grassy edge of the cliff, glancing down occasionally at the shingle far below. Then, at his feet there was a startled gasp, so unexpected that he almost tripped and fell. A figure rose from a ledge just below the edge of the cliff, and a white face glimmered at him.

"Who's that?" said a frightened voice. "Damn it, why do you walk so quiet?" After a moment he recognized her.

"So it's you," he said. "You must be frozen."

"Yes," she said, "I was just sitting and thinking. I hadn't realized it was so cold," she clambered stiffly up on to the grass and they walked together down the slope of the cliff, aimlessly.

"How did you get on with Steve?" he asked.

"Steve?" she said. "Oh! Oh, yes. He wanted to meet me on Friday." She laughed harshly. "Friday," she said again. "Only to-morrow comes before Friday."

The ground levelled off beneath their feet. They climbed a breakwater and found themselves among the sand-dunes that back the strand. Their shoes slipped on spiky rushes and wiry marram-grass that topped the dunes, and their feet floundered in the soft sandy hollows. Here the breeze was above their heads. They came to a bowl-shaped hollow, a few yards across, where the sand was streaked with grass like hair on a bald head.

"I'm tired," she said, sitting down and curling her feet under her. "Let's rest a while".

"Smoke?" said Joe, pulling out a battered packet of cigarettes.

"Thanks," she said. The match flared up with an unexpectedly loud sound and she closed her eyes against the glare. The cigarette wavered and burned unevenly. Then the matchflame quivered and died, and there were only the two glowing coals in the growing darkness. She looked up at his face as it was illuminated by the warm pulsing light. She leaned back on one arm and then yelped suddenly.

"Something bit me," she said, in a tone of terror. Joe took a swift pace forwards and, leaning a hand on her shoulder, looked where her fingers had rested.

"It's only a sea-thistle," he said, laughing. He struck another match, and in the leaping yellow light she saw the pale streaky jade stem, the wickedly-spined grey-green leaves, the wine-coloured savage blossom, delicate-looking as bone china and tough as steel.

"Oh." she said, "It's beautiful!" She touched the blossom incautiously and yelped again, for each soft-seeming pink tendril was a needle-sharp spine. "But unfriendly," she said sadly, and looked at Joe again.

He stood there, looking down at her, the cigarette smouldering away between his fingers. A little gust of wind, barbed with sand, came frisking over the dunes, and she shivered under his fingers.

"You are cold," he said, straightening up. "Wait a moment." He remembered something he had glimpsed in the matchlight. He searched around at the base of the sand-dune and unearthed a couple of pieces of driftwood. He crumpled up some scraps of blown newspaper, broke driftwood in fragments over his knee, and built a small fire which blazed up rapidly. He dragged along some more pieces of wood from the next hollow and fed them into the flames. As they burned away, he kicked them further into the fire. The sand grew warm and they leaned back against the slope of the dune, barely an arm-stretch apart. Waves grumbled on shingle somewhere far away, and the night wind whispered above. The darkness poised itself and waited above the bowl of firelight.

"I remember doing this'" said Joe, 'when we were kids. We were smoking on the sly and we came here one night with a packet of cigarettes and found we had only one match, so we had to light a fire to keep us going for the night. Just as well, too. January it was, as far as I remember."

"Adventurous childhood you had," said Iris, laughing. "All boys together. Give you a packet of cigarettes and you wanted nothing more. And I suppose you threw stones at the Girl Guides' camp."

"Yes," said Joe, surprised, "we did that, and there was hell to pay afterwards. How did you guess?"

"I have the second sight, of course. I can foretell the future, too. Boys will be boys, and girls will be – " she checked herself. She leaned forwards and threw the stub of the cigarette into the fire. A piece of wood fell over and the flames leaped up. Her eyes glittered and her teeth shone very white. "Damn it, I wish – ." She took up a fistful of sand and let it sift slowly through her fingers. She glanced at him, and in the flicker of firelight he could not be certain of the expression on her face.

"I'm sorry I came and I'm sorry to be going back again. I don't know what way I am." She stared into the fire again.

Joe kicked his heels into the sand, digging out a little hollow. He squirmed his shoulders against the dune until a trickle of sand ran down his collar. He looked at his hand, lying so still beside him. He looked at Iris's fire-bright profile a couple of feet away. He raised his hand, slowly, as though shoulder and elbow were frozen stiff. She stared, motionless, into the flames. He stretched out his hand toward her shoulder, but it was just beyond reach. The few inches of firelit darkness were a barrier which he could not summon the courage to cross. Moments crawled by, and his hand slowly dropped to his side again. She cupped her elbows in her palms and hunched her shoulders. The fire crackled and he gazed into its golden caverns until his eyes were tired.

His head snapped forward suddenly and jerked him awake. Iris was rocking from side to side and crooning what sounded like a Scottish lullaby. She looked sidelong, mockingly, at him.

"Sleepy, poor boy?" she asked.

"No," said Joe, "no. Just dizzy from the fire." He leaned forward and pushed timber into the flames. The light leaped up. Her eyes smiled at him. her lips curved. Now, he thought; what's stopping me; where's the harm in a bit of fun; kiss her, you fool. Then she laughed suddenly at the sight of him there against the fire, neck twisted awkwardly, brow furrowed in decision.

"Have one of mine," she said, holding out a cigarette packet. "As the farmer said when he came in and found his son at grips with the maid, 'You'll be smoking next.' Don't look so dismal. You don't have to go back tomorrow." The moment was gone. He pulled a red ember from the fire, scorching his fingers, and lit the cigarettes. There was a chill feeling under his ribs that the fire's warmth could not reach. After a moment she gave a little choking sound as though she had swallowed a puff of smoke, then began to hum again. She stood up, brushing the sand from her skirt, and he rolled over on one elbow to watch her.

"Want to go home?" he asked.

"Oh, no," she said, "not on my last night. Not on your life, boy. No, don't get up," she said, as he began to scramble to his feet, "you stay there and I'll be right back." She flicked the cigarette butt into the flames and stood there for a moment, looking down at him, the firelight sending red shadows chasing over her face so that her expression was hidden.

"Where – ?" began Joe.

"Don't be so rude, little boy," she said gaily. "You wait there now until I come back." She opened her hand slowly and dropped beside him on the sand the remains of the sea-thistle which she had torn from its roots. Its sharp spines, some of them broken in the struggle to uproot it, were tipped with a few tiny drops of blood. He looked down at the thistle, unable to think of anything to say, and when he raised his head again she was already outside the range of the firelight. For a few moments he could hear her muffled footsteps in the sand-dune, then for a while the crunch and shift of shingle and then nothing at all but the cold night wind in the rushes.

Far out towards the horizon he could see the dim, milky glimmer of waves breaking on the strand, but everything else was lost in the darkness. He slid back down into the hollow and waited patiently, resting on one elbow, staring into the fire until at length it seemed an immense torch-lit street where a silent procession marched between huge dark buildings. The buildings wavered like flags in a light air and loomed slowly, slowly larger, growing nearer and nearer until at long, long last they towered toppling over him.

He woke, stiff and half-frozen, a long time later. The moon was up, and by its position he judged it to be well after midnight. A thread of smoke rose up into the night air from the fire's last embers. He was quite alone. He rolled over slowly and painfully and something clawed through his shirt and into his chest. It was the battered remnant of the thistle. He got to his feet and looked back over the desolate empty spaces of the strand, herring-boned with black shadow, then he began to stumble stiffly homewards over the moonlit dunes. He carried the thistle, unthinkingly crushed in his palm.

[vi]

His sleep was short and restless, disturbed by strange dreams of galloping white horses with black manes, which raced threateningly towards him down streets of tall houses and turned away, prancing, at the last moment. He woke, half-choked, to find the pillow on top of his face and the blankets strewn about the floor. The window was open, and the sound of bird-song came in to greet him. He went over and looked out at the estuary.

It was not long after dawn. The western sky was still grey. Nothing moved, except the slow, oily ripples of the tide near flood. A cold, green-gold light lapped everything about, solidly, like a layer of Venetian glass; the anchored boats, drifted by the aimless eddies, pointed at random. On top of the water-bailiffs' cream-painted launch a seagull perched one-legged and lazily preened its feathers. Far out on the other side of the channel a great salmon came soaring and shuddering out of the water like a great electric spark. The ripples widened out, breaking mirrored images of sand, rocks, trees, buoys, boats into trembling shafts of green and gold and brown. Joe took a deep, deep, peaceful breath and turned away, running his fingers through his tousled hair.

He picked his clothes from where he had dropped them in a heap at the foot of the bed, shrugged his way into them, and went down the stairs on tiptoe, barefoot. He picked up a hand-line, and the bag of crabs, closed the door softly behind him; a moment while he struggled into a pair of broken tennis-shoes, then he crossed the road, climbed the breakwater, and dropped down to the beach.

An hour later he was still knee-deep in the icy wavelets, feeling the sand dribbling away with the undertow from beneath his feet. The sun at last had cleared the sea wall and was pleasantly warm on his back. The straining line, stretching towards the edge of the smoothly-humped channel, tingled pleasantly on his finger from the pulsing of the tide. He whistled cheerfully and shifted his weight from one foot to the other, looking with satisfaction at the empty shore and the wide, empty sea.

There came a succession of soft tugs at the line. He slackened his grip slightly and let the cord slide slowly between forefinger and thumb. A yard of line had gone, by fractions of slow inches. He tightened his fingers, felt the live movement still there, and jerked his wrist back. The line jumped and sawed about as he heaved it in, careless now in what confusion the coils might drop. A bar of vibrant olive-silver came threshing in, gills gaping, the spiky back-fin erect and ready to slash.

Joe ran splashing into the strand, dragging the bass yards clear of the water's edge. He left it there for a moment and came back with a chunk of rock. With one foot pressing the spines to rest, he measured the distance carefully and struck the fish on the small dark patch at the back of its head. Its gills opened and closed, it quivered violently, the olive tinge of its sides turned to blue and then to cold silver, and it lay still.

Joe twisted out the hook and happily lifted the bass with a finger through its gills. He dabbled it in the edge of the waves to wash the sand away, and looked at it proudly. Eight pounds, give or take a few ounces. It was moments like this that made fishing worth a man's whole life and exclusive devotion.

Tenderly he levered up the great back fin, which came up like a plume, translucent, ribbed with needle-sharp spines, gleaming in the sunlight. He touched the spines, cautiously, but sea-water had numbed his fingers and he pressed too hard before he felt the stab of pain. A tiny droplet of blood glittered on the spine like a splinter of ruby. A cloud seemed to pass over the sun, and the splashed patches became noticeably chill. The gold had gone out of the morning and the sea was grey.

He wrinkled his forehead and looked though almost-closed lids at the sun, estimating time. Nearly eight o'clock. A quarter of an hour to spare, at best. He dragged in the coils of line and crammed them anyhow, tangled and weed-festooned, into the sack with the crabs, and ran away along the beach. The tide had reached the corner of the tennis court wall, but he splashed heedlessly through the shin-deep water. He pulled the latchcord of his own door, threw the sack in a corner, grabbed an old newspaper to wrap around the bass, and raced out again, letting the door bang behind him. He ran along the streets of the old town, his shoes and his soaked trousers leaving trails of seawater on the grey pavements.

When he came as far as the lighthouse at the top of the hill, his heart was pounding in his ribs and his side hurt. Steam rose in great clouds beyond the station buildings. No belated travellers were in sight. He kept on running, unsteadily. The platform clock, unbelievably, showed still four minutes to the hour. He waited a moment until his breath was more or less under control, then went through the barrier and walked along beside the train.

She was sitting in a corner seat of an empty compartment, reading a film-magazine. He tapped the glass. She looked up, half-smiled, and opened the window.

"Well," she said, "if it isn't the Boy Scout himself. The last time I saw you, you were snoring fine and loud." Joe, startled and disbelieving, stared at her. Jest or earnest? What matter now. She laughed abruptly. "Lucky there isn't anyone around to hear us. Your reputation would be ruined. And all for nothing."

"I've got something for you," said Joe. "Sorry the parcel is so clumsy, but I hadn't time..."

"Well, well," she said. She lifted the corner of the newspaper and peered in. Her eyes widened and she gave a muffled snort that might have been a laugh or a sob. "Well, now I've seen everything. Fish. Thanks. It was a nice thought. Now I'll have something to remember you by."

They looked at one another wordlessly, she resting her elbows on the frame of the window and stroking the red scratches on the palms of her hands, Joe leaning one shoulder against the side of the carriage, his wet flannels sticking to his shins. Stray spurts of steam curled up from under the footboard and drifted between their faces. The station-master came out of the waiting- room, looked at the clock and went in again.

"Will you be coming back?" asked Joe. "When will you be coming back. I mean?"

"Did you ever hear the story about the Trans-Siberian Railway?" she asked. "No?" She took a deep breath, looked away up the line, and began to pick at a blister of paint on the window frame.

"Well, there was this Russian soldier and the Russian girl that got on the train in Moscow and they had the carriage all to themselves. A fortnight later, when they had got to the middle of nowhere, the soldier says: 'It is cold.' And a fortnight after that, when they were passing through Omsk, the girl says: 'Yes, it is cold.' And a week later, when they had left Tomsk, the soldier says: 'Would you like the window closed?' And a week after that, when they got to Irkutsk, the girl says: 'Yes, I would like the window closed.' And a fortnight later, when they were still three weeks away from Vladivostok, the soldier stands up slowly and says: 'Enough of this love talk: take off your clothes!"'

Iris looked down at him unsmilingly. "They got married in Vladivostok and lived miserably ever after. Isn't that a nice story?"

Joe began to say something, but his words were lost in the deafening roar of escaping steam. The station-master came through the barrier with his furled green flag ready. He looked from his watch to the clock and back again. Joe put his hand, fingers still pallid and pasty from the sea-water on the window frame.

"Well?" he asked, and managed a grin.

"Enough of this love-talk," she said. "I'm not coming back. I'm off to Vladivostok in the morning. You've missed the train."

The station-master waved his flag, the train shuddered and groaned into movement. A great cloud of steam billowed up between them, hiding her face, and he stepped back. When the steam cleared away he saw her face at the window, already beyond reach, black tousled hair framing pale features. Her hand waved cheerfully. He raised his arm to shoulder level, then, after a few moments, let it drop limply to his side again. The train went round the curve and she was lost to his sight.

He turned and went across the station-yard, dragging his toes through the drifted sand. He went through the gateway and looked out at a grey tumbled sea and a grey sky. There were good fish in it yet, or so they said. A stout man came trotting towards the gate, carrying a suitcase and a raincoat, breathless, red-faced, worried-looking. He gestured wildly as he came.

"I'm sorry," said Joe politely, "I'm afraid you've missed the train." He left the stout man standing forlornly in the gateway, and, shoes squelching desolately, went slowly home.

[vii]

Nowadays (as Sir Thomas Malory noted) *men cannot love seven nights but they must have all their desires, that love may not endure by reason: for where they be soon accorded, and hasty heat, soon it cooleth. This is no stability, but the old love was not so. Men and women could love together seven years, and no wanton lusts were between them, and then was love truth and faithfulness. And lo in likewisse was used love in king Arthurs days.*

Nowadays, unhappily, one has not seven years to spare.

PART III

EPHEMERA

ON A BLUE NOTE

Why do I dodge, prevaricate or postpone the question of polishing shoes? It is, after all, a pastime, a hobby, a minor and satisfying art in itself. I even enjoy it, when it comes to the point, which it rarely does. I remember one extremely comfortable pair of shoes which had begun to crack in an interesting cobweb pattern due to lack of polish and subjection to watersplashes from the front wheel of a bicycle, but were, as I thought, good for many a winter yet. One day I observed that the cracks in the leather were turning from fawn to grey: not until rain had started did I realise that I had been observing my own socks. My wife pointed out, despairingly, that she had told me so.

Bachelors can dodge the polish brush indefinitely. Not so the family man. About once a month I find myself, in the dismal small hours when everyone else is in bed, tackling the family shoes: the clog-like pair which my small daughter personally insisted on selecting, with a piece mysteriously sliced out of the welt; the conical pair, as broad as they're long, belonging to my two-year-old son's square feet; no wonder he walks like a mechanical toy, to the delight of old ladies; my own immense dumpers, still happily intact though battered. Soon I suppose my younger son will abandon knitted boots and join the queue. But my wife won't trust me with her shoes.

Night thoughts, with a gas-jet singing loudly in the

sleeping house. I feel old, and I'm now myself one of the "older generation". I remember reading of a man who possessed five hundred pairs of shoes, and a special room for storing them and cleaning them with polishes specially blended for himself alone. That man would have appealed to my father, whose great delight was a line of muddy shoes awaiting transformation – he even kept a special blunt penknife for preliminary scraping. I think he included shoes which had long since been abandoned, hiding them at the bottom of the cupboard with brushes and dusters – at any rate there always seemed to be many more shoes than the family could possibly wear.

It was on such an occasion, before I'd read "Handy Andy" for myself, that he told me about Tom Connors' Cat. As you may remember, Tom Connors was measuring his children for shoes to be bought at the fair when the cat spoke up and said "Tom Connors, will you buy me a pair of shoes?" The measurements were being taken in the traditional manner, by notching a tally-stick with a big knife, and the resultant confusion caused the youngest Connors to lose a toe. My father remembered having seen shoes bought in such a manner, shoes which were interchangeable with neither left nor right; no nonsense about X-ray fitting in those days.

So a chapter in past history' is alive for me. What, of all that I've told my children from time to time, will they recall in their turn?

They'll never know the delight of running barefoot in a country road in summer, soft dust whooshing in puffs between their toes: there are no country roads anymore. Will such vanished delights of my own childhood seem real to them? Or will they recall something that appeared completely unimportant in the telling? My bet is that they'll remember little.

A last flick of the duster, then store away the brushes and throw away the tin. Must buy more polish tomorrow. Where are those espadrilles which I bought for 1/6 in Clermont-Ferrand? Did the bin-man finally get them when my back was turned? I will wear spats, and tan the soles of my feet, and start a new fashion, and hire famous artists to paint miniatures on my big toe. Then, perhaps, my children will remember me.

OLIVERMANSHIP

A best-selling novelist in a recent interview admitted to starting his career by hammering out short stories on an "old Oliver typewriter". I'll wager ten to one it used two-tone ribbons, that it wasn't just any old Oliver, but that freelancer's friend, that skeleton in every writer's closet, the cheapest of all practical writing instruments, the Oliver Standard.

The Oliver Company (I assume it's the same company) still makes typewriters – good ones, but the last Oliver Standard was manufactured about forty years ago.* It was, however, quite imperishable, and therefore so much outlasted its time that it could eventually be bought, in good working order, for the price of a good fountain pen.

It looked more like a piece of agricultural machinery than a typewriter. The base was an impressive construction of cast iron, standing a couple of hands clear of the table. The carriage, of extreme weight, shifted in two directions, producing strong muscles in the operator, while the rock-hard roller caused calluses on his fingertips. The type-bars were two long horseshoes, pivoted at each end, rising in two banks like organ-pipes at either side of the machine, the top inadequately protected by a metal band. However, the keys didn't need much protection: the modern typewriter is a job

* *This piece was written in 1954*

for the jeweller, but the Oliver Standard, true to its appearance, needed only the occasional services of a blacksmith.

Since the keys descended vertically on the roller, paper had to be inserted from the back. With a worn machine, it was possible to insert paper, spin the roller rapidly, and produce no apparent result – except the marvellous disappearance of one's prospective typescript. The expert Oliverman, of course, knew that the machine had guzzled the paper into a tight ball and wadded it somewhere in its cast-iron basement. When inserting the next sheet he took a firm grip on its free end, like a housewife feeding a blanket into a mangle, and the Oliver would obey, recognising the master's touch.

It has been impossible, for the last twenty years at least, to buy a ribbon made for an Oliver Standard, which used a weird little wooden bobbin instead of the present neat spool. So the Oliver-man had to search around for a ribbon of the right size and wind it painfully, with sad results to his fingers, onto his little hoard of bobbins. Thereafter, whenever he was in the throes of inspiration, the ribbon would usually spring loose from its moorings and form a cat's cradle around the keys.

The pause while the mess was disentangled came as a relief to the inhabitants, not alone of the house, but of the entire neighbourhood, for the sound of an Oliver in full gallop was the envy of Lambeg drummers.

Admittedly I once saw an Oliver (belonging to one of our more promising young playwrights) which by some freak had been preserved in showroom condition, though it was not exempt from the universal bobbin trouble.

—~—

My brother's machine, which turned out millions of words in its time, was more typical. The carriage-return spring had rusted and broken. Spare parts were, needless to say, unobtainable, but the brother solved the problem with a few feet of fishing line, complete with a two-pound sinker, tied to the carriage and hanging over the edge of the table. Inelegant perhaps, but pleasing to the Oliverman.

My own Oliver had lain in a damp cupboard in a holiday resort for a couple of generations before I bought it. I padded it round with several pullovers and wedged it into a large strong suitcase, but when I was changing trains the machine tore its way out of the suitcase and landed heavily on the platform. Suitcase and pullovers were irreparably damaged, but the Oliver was quite unhurt.

It lasted me for seven or eight years, until I graduated to a modern machine with no vices and little character. Incidentally, in common with most of its marque, my specimen had keys on which the letters had long been worn completely away, so that I acquired a certain facility in touch-typing – of a kind!

I wish I knew where that Oliver is now. Perhaps it is in the possession of some future best-seller-writer, who labours over it and swears at it as he blows on his numbed fingertips. But he'll smile as I do, at the memory in ten years' time, by which time it will probably be working for yet another young writer. For, like the best prose, the Oliver Standard is an enduring monument to its maker, who builded better than he knew.

GEORGE FITZMORRIS: (SKETCH FOR A PORTRAIT)*

A merry little man, you might say: a man who carries his years lightly and seems not to have a care in the world. He appears to have little liking for the veneer, the surface glitter of civilisation, for cinemas and lounge bars: but in his favourite position with his elbow on the counter of a pub and a glass of stout in his free hand, he will talk entertainingly on a variety of matters – of the noble hooded cloaks handed down from generation to generation in Valentia and Bandon, of fairs and funerals in Killorglin and Abbeyfeale, of the decline of "visiting houses" and the old way of life in his native Kerry, and of the great days of the old-time music hall. Perhaps, from his reminiscences of Dublin at the turn of the century, you will gather that he knew the leading figures of the literary revival, but as to his own story and his own part in the revival, it is as easy to interview an oyster.

This is the man of whom Ernest Boyd said in 1918: "George Fitzmaurice has imagination and style of a sufficiently personal quality to give him rank as the greatest folk-dramatist since the death of Synge" (*The Contemporary Drama of Ireland*). Against the background of the Abbey playwrights of that time, it was a reasonable claim, but

* *Published in Irish Writing, 1951*

unfortunately it was not borne out: lack of appreciation, misguidance of his talents, other causes, made him drift away from the theatre. His occasional one-act plays have, since 1923, been published in *The Dublin Magazine* on their literary merits, for their dramatic qualities, and with one exception, were small; they were plays in appearance only. I believe that the loss to the Irish theatre of his potential talents was considerable.

George Fitzmaurice, eldest son of a farmer, was born some time between 1880 and 1890, in Kilcara, near Duagh in North Kerry, a land of abrupt mountains and small blue lakes, a land which still held a remnant of the ancient Gaelic civilisation. Of his early life I know nothing, but around the turn of the century he was working as a clerk in the Congested Districts Board. He was described by his companions as a sociable character, "a great man to drink a pint," but one who was given to day-dreaming, and rambling off on his own at times. This was the period of the Irish Literary Revival. Literature and theatre were in the air. "Everybody," says Fitzmaurice, "was writing plays." He wrote a full length comedy and sent it to the Abbey in 1907, the year of *The Playboy*. Judging by the construction of his plays, I should say that his models and examples were no more than a knowledge of Shakespeare, a memory of touring companies playing *Arrah-na-pogue* and *Con the Shaughraun,* and his own fertile imagination. Besides this, he had a flair for dialogue, based on the Kerry idiom, which gladdens the ear and ennobles a character.

It might be as well to deal with the question of dialect style at this point. It was said of Synge that he merely wrote down what he heard through a crack in the floor of a loft, and Fitzmaurice even went as far as to say of himself: "sure anybody who could write down the sayings of Kerry people could fool anyone he was a poet." That, however, is only half the story: for the other half, for the artistic selection and creation which brings a "natural" line to life, I must introduce an unexpected and impartial witness – Raymond Chandler, whose remarks on style have universal application. In the course of some comments on the masters of the American detective story, he said: "Dashiell Hammet put these people down on paper as they really are, and he made them talk and think in the language they customarily used for these purposes. He had style, but his audience didn't know it, because it was in a language not supposed to be capable of these refinements. They thought they were getting a good meaty melodrama written in the kind of lingo they imagined they spoke themselves. It was in a sense, but it was much more. All language begins with speech, and the speech of common men at that, but when it develops to the point of becoming a literary medium, it only looks like speech." Change a word here and there, and that passage could be applied to any of Fitzmaurice's plays. For the sheer delight of his language, if for no other reason, his plays are worth preserving.

The full-length play which he sent to the Abbey was *The Country Dressmaker*, a sparkling comedy. It was accepted by them, and produced on 3rd October, 1907. In the policy of short runs and no revivals which was the practice of the Abbey at the time, it was something of a success. It may be a coincidence that Fitzmaurice resigned from the Congested Districts Board during the same year, but I think there is a connection. At this period it is possible that, not having tasted discouragement, he hoped to devote his life to writing: it is fairly certain that he had strong views on his own work at this time (as a story of an argument with

Yeats over the cutting of a line of dialogue would seem to prove) in contrast to his present remarkably casual attitude to productions of his plays.

During the following year, the Abbey presented his second play, *The Pie Dish,* a very fine one-act tragedy. Its reception must have been a terrible shock to the young dramatist. "For some reason which cannot be explained," said Andrew E. Malone, "this play was always received with hilarity in the Abbey Theatre. In no other Irish play is there elaborated the theme of the frustration of the artist in Ireland, and the struggle between the Paganism of the artist and his Christian environment. It is probable that the complete misinterpretation of this little play did much to retard the growth of appreciation which its author deserved." And Ernest Boyd said '"This curious little piece in one act, which failed to secure the sympathies of an audience already in search of digestive amusement, was soon forgotten on the accession of the new regime of imitative peasant playwrights. It is not surprising, therefore, that he should have waited seven years before publishing his first play."

I think that the "inexplicable reason" referred to by Malone is clearly explained by Boyd's observation. Even at that early date, the Abbey audiences were determined to be amused. If their favourite comedians were appearing, the play was a riotous success, whatever the subject. The shock to a young and sincere author must have been brutal. There is an interesting confirmation of this point. *The Challenge,* by Winifred Letts, was produced at the Abbey on 14 October 1909; it was her second play for the Abbey and she was rather proud of it. In a recent article, 'Early Days at the Abbey', she says: "Yeats and Lady Gregory had approved the idea of it –

two old men who fight a duel in an old Dublin house over a wrong that one of them has entirely forgotten. It was intended for a tragedy, but the audience decided at once that Arthur Sinclair, Fred O'Donovan and Kerrigan must be engaged in a comedy, whatever they might say. As each appeared there were shrieks of laughter and the laughter barely ceased as one old man fell dead from over-excitement when the clock signalled for them to shoot. As the author, I could have prayed for the boards to rise up and cover me. Not even the sympathy of Yeats and Lady Gregory could salve the hurt of that absurd but miserable moment." Winifred Letts never again wrote a play for the Abbey.

It is hardly surprising that Fitzmaurice wrote no more for some time: possibly he went back to Kerry for a while. About 1910 he rejoined CDB, now the Land Commission, and three years later (April, 1913) his curious one-act play, *The Magic Glasses,* was produced. In this play, he took refuge from misinterpretation in fantasy, in an allegory of the frustrated artist, the theme of *The Pie Dish* again. Ernest Boyd points out a resemblance between *The Magic Glasses* and Ibsen's *The Wild Duck* – "the loft to which Jaymoney retires in order to enjoy the fairy music reminds us of the garret in *The Wild Duck,* within whose shelter the old grandfather was transported to a world of imagination."

This is not the only curious point about this curious play (which Harry Clarke chose as one of the representatives for his famous Geneva Window, commissioned by the League of Nations). Some time ago, I came upon a Japanese play – *The Madman on the Roof,* by Kan Kikuchi – which was almost identical in plot and treatment to *The Magic Glasses.* I asked Professor Glen Hughes, the translator, about it, and he wrote: "I agree with you that there is an extraordinary similarity between this play and Kikuchi's. I believe however that there is a possibility of Kan Kikuchi having seen the Fitzmaurice piece and taken his idea from it. The Madman was first published in 1919 and produced at the Imperial Theatre, Tokyo, in 1920. I think it was written shortly before publication. Why the author set his action as far back as 1900, I do not know. The Japanese are great thieves. Many of their plays are literally stolen from European and American works. Before they had contact with our drama they even stole from each other. They did not even consider this a reprehensible practice. You may be sure that if a copy of *The Magic Glasses*, which I note was published in 1914, managed to fall into the hands of Kikuchi, there is no mystery at all in the similarity between the plays."

It is an interesting speculation, suggesting that the circulation of Fitzmaurice's published works was far-flung, but in the absence of any further evidence, it must remain a speculation.

With the production of *The Magic Glasses*, a pattern begins to emerge – a slight encouragement, followed by a burst of playwriting industry (the incentive for writing *The Magic Glasses* was a revival of *The Country Dressmaker* in 1912): or discouragement, followed by a long silence. The pattern recurs throughout Fitzmaurice's work. In the next two years he wrote two more plays, *The Magic Glasses* having met with no opposition, if no outright success. These plays were the one-act fantasy, *The Dandy Dolls*, and the full-length play, *The Moonlighters*, a major work by the dramatic standards of that period.

The Dandy Dolls was not produced until 1945. And in January 1949, A. J. Leventhal writes in *The Dublin Magazine*: "George Fitzmaurice had to wait well over thirty years for the realisation on the stage of his play, *The Moonlighters*. It was not, as one might have expected, the Abbey Theatre that paid this belated tribute to one of the most imaginative dramatists of the revival, but an amateur company." The five plays which Fitzmaurice had written at that time were published by Maunsel and Co. in a collected edition in 1914 (they had also published *The Magic Glasses*, on its own, earlier the same year). The volume met with small sales. In a few years, the firm broke up, the unbound stocks of Five Plays being taken over by Veritas Ltd, and later by Talbot Press, who issued four of the plays singly in blue paper covers. Discouragement was complete. For twenty years, with minor exceptions, Fitzmaurice was a forgotten voice.

Then, *The Country Dressmaker* was revived by the Abbey in 1942. Austin Clarke's Lyric Theatre Company produced *The Dandy Dolls* for the first time in December, 1945, and followed it with a revival of *The Magic Glasses* in 1946. *The Moonlighters* was again under consideration by the Abbey in 1947, but the project collapsed. Thus encouraged. Fitzmaurice wrote two further one-act plays: *There are Tragedies and Tragedies*, (published in *The Dublin Magazine*, September, 1948) and *One Evening Gleam* (*The Dublin Magazine*, January 1949). He had retired from the Land Commission shortly before the war and since then had been living in Kerry. His lack of contact with the theatre over the long period since 1923 is well shown in these plays, which have little of dramatic interest, and will probably be remembered only by those few, who, like myself, believe that Fitzmaurice's work is of lasting importance.

The revival of interest in his work was reflected in a production of *The Magic Glasses* by an amateur company – Earlsfort Players – in September, 1947. A year later, this group presented *The Moonlighters* for the first time, as already noted. It was a laudable, but perhaps over-ambitious, venture, and the critical reception was mixed. Most authorities said that the play showed its age, and was rather confusing; *The Dublin Magazine* however, in the review already mentioned, pointed out that a professional production would have disguised the obvious faults in the play, and given full scope to the genius and vitality behind it. "The action is wedded to a dialogue that shows a mastery of what used to be called the 'Anglo-Irish' idiom, and which, in the mouths of trained actors, would have smoothed, if it did not entirely eliminate, the roughnesses of plot; the imaginative phrase deftly delivered could have shaded some of the seeming crudities of the amateur interpretation; not that Liam Miller, who both produced the play and designed the setting, was without feeling for the dramatist's purpose; it was inevitable that the untutored cast could not rise to the demands inherent in the text."

The list of productions of all those plays by Fitzmaurice which had more than a literary interest, was completed by the presentation of *The Linnaun Shee* by the Lyric Theatre Company in May, 1949 (followed within the week by another revival of *The Country Dressmaker*, which met with unqualified success). *The Linnaun Shee* is a gem, possibly the best one-act play ever written by Fitzmaurice. Published in *The Dublin Magazine* in 1924, it is alone among the plays after *The Moonlighters* in avoiding an exaggeration of artificially academic language on the part of one character or another. It was completely forgotten for a quarter of a century. Andrew E. Malone's definitive work, *The Irish Drama*, published in 1929, overlooks this play, while referring to an amusing trifle called 'The Green Stone' (*The Dublin Magazine*, 1926) in which he claims to see an indication "that George Fitzmaurice may one day give to Ireland a romantic drama such as Ibsen gave to Norway in Peer Gynt." This hope, unfortunately, remains unfulfilled.

The list of Fitzmaurice's plays is completed by the one act comedy, 'Twixt the Giltinans and the Carmodys. produced at the Abbey in 1923, and eventually published in *The Dublin Magazine* in 1943. It is an extension of the match-making tangles and the stock figure of the returned Yank in The Country Dressmaker, but without the original touches which gave his first play its brilliance and humanity. Its cursory plot and slapdash characterisation doomed it to artistic failure, in spite of its occasional passages of delightful dialogue. "It may be," said Malone, "that in disgust at the treatment that had been given to his finer efforts he had decided to tickle the groundlings with this play. But even in this tangle of families there is no descent to the farcical." The compromise, however, proved no gain, and was artistic suicide. With the sole exception of *The Linnaun Shee,* Fitzmaurice's work since 1914 remains of small importance, although it is possible that if any encouragement had been shown him at that critical period, he might have become one of the more important names in the history of Irish theatre.

His present reputation rests solidly on the two full-length plays. *The Country Dressmaker*, and *The Moonlighters*. The former, as already indicated, has always been something of a success, and has been frequently revived. The plot is simple and universal, telling of Julia Shea, who has spent her life reading novelettes, and taking her views of ideal life from them: how she has built up a romantic idea of Pats Conner, gone to make his fortune in America, because her neighbours have tricked her into believing that he will return to marry her: how Pats returns and keeps up the deception, at first as a joke and then in all sincerity; how Julia at first rejects him, because he does not tally with her romantic ideal; how they are further separated by the machinations of a neighbour with marriageable daughters: and how, in the end, the complications are overcome, to the satisfaction of all concerned. It is a heartwarming play, and the character of Julia Shea, the dressmaker, who is silly and impulsive, yet possesses a strange dignity, is a pleasure to meet. "This perfect comedy of rural manners," was Ernest Boyd's considered judgement.

The Moonlighters is a more ambitious play, but is not as smooth in construction. It deals with the troubled times of the Land War, and contrasts the characters of Peter Guerin, a "reformed" Fenian, and his son Eugene, a fiery patriot in words at least, against a background of the under-cover revolutionary activity of the time – activity which sometimes degenerates into mere faction-fights, and at other times was diverted to private vengeance under the guise of patriotism.

The keynote of the play is that there is no special pleading on behalf of one character more than another. Malachi Cantillon, the gombeen man; Maura Driscoll and Breeda Carmody, whose love for Eugene and his friend Tom involves themselves in tragedy; Synan, the ill-fated young captain of the Moonlighters; Big William Cantillon, the grabber, and Morisheen Lucy, whose land is grabbed – they are all living human beings, who carry the evidence of their own truth. We feel that these characters really existed, that the play is a true picture of the country at that time. The interest continually shifts from one character to another, which explains the apparently disjointed effect of the play.

It is a poetical documentary, so to speak, with neither conventional hero nor "minor" characters.

A certain authority on Irish history told me that he objected strongly to *The Moonlighters,* because it was grossly unfair to the ideals of the secret revolutionary organisation. A discussion of this point, involving history and politics, would be out of place here, but I cannot understand how anyone could carry away such an opinion from reading the play. For my own part, I can never read it without a catch in my throat, and I agree wholeheartedly with Malone's comment in 1929: "Why this play should never have been staged when so many that were in every way inferior were produced at the Abbey is incredible to everyone who knows it in the printed version." As we have seen, it was staged eventually. Perhaps, some day, it will be presented as it deserves to be.

Of Fitzmaurice's one-act plays, five may be grouped under Ernest Boyd's phrase – "they have neither the style nor the substance which would repay an attempt to summarise them." These are, in chronological order, *The Dandy Dolls* , *Twixt the Giltinans and the Carmodys, The Green Stone, There are Tragedies and Tragedies,* and *One Evening Gleam*. I admit frankly that I am puzzled by *The Dandy Dolls* ; Boyd sees it as "an exercise in pure fancy, situated beyond the limitations of human experience ... the narrative of a widely grotesque struggle against the forces of the supernatural ... the Grey Man and the Hag's Son who steal the windpipes from the throats of Roger Carmody's dolls are creatures of the same race as the Trolls of Ibsen."

The really important one-act plays are the strange trio which remain for consideration – *The Pie Dish, The Magic Glasses,* and *The Linnaun Shee;* their importance, however, has not been generally recognised. I think there is a clearlink between the three, disguised by the element of fantasy in the later plays. Fitzmaurice's fantasy, as said earlier, is a refuge from misinterpretation. Some people have observed this fact, as a passing reference by Austin Clarke in another connection indicates – "Our modern dramatic fantasies began forty years ago with those symbolic comedies by George Fitzmaurice, *The Dandy Dolls* and *The Magic Glasses* – wonder-plays which, like all true treasure, remain hidden from us until we dream for the third time" In this quotation, "symbolic" is the operative word; the symbols are obscure and generally overlooked. That some see their significance is shown by a sentence from Benedict Kiely's review of the recent *Linnaun Shee* production – "Fitzmaurice's play, written many years ago and now produced for the first time, survived some awkward opening moments, to attain to an entrancing beauty and terror and mystery." This is a striking statement about a play which others summed up as a whimsical comedy.

The Pie Dish is the tragedy of Leum Donohue, who has devoted his life to the modelling of an ornamental pie dish, the final and complete expression of his artistic soul: "It's my heart's blood is in you, my pie dish! 'Tis little more will crown it, Eugene, and then it's for old Moll of Carraweina you will go, and Black Jack of Scartaglen, and old Teigue of Glounaneinta – to come and see it in all its glory. Them is all that's left of the friends of my youth, and 'tis a lot are gone and cold surely, since I first gave under making my pie dish twenty years ago." The work is interrupted by the approach of death. He prays for time to finish, but his prayer is unanswered. He calls on the devil to give him time. The dish falls from his hand and is shattered, and he dies. The priest's comment, as he takes up a piece of the dish, is: "What folly and vanity there do be in this short world! But what was in all this at all? What was in this at all?" The summing-up is in Eugene's words, "it's in bits now, and what it was or what it wasn't no one will be a pin's point the wiser for ever more."

The Magic Glasses tells how Jaymony Shanahan's family were disturbed and fearful of the good name from Jaymony's habit of retiring to the top loft, entertaining himself with strange music, and gazing into a set of magic glasses given to him by a mysterious woman many years before. They enlist the aid of a local bonesetter and quack, one Morgan Quille. Jaymony relates the wonderful sights to be seen in the three sets of glasses. Quille prescribes unusual and complicated cures. For a while the cure seems to take effect, but Jaymony relapses into his old ways, and dies suddenly in confusion and mystery, so that the last state of the family is worse than the first.

The Linnaun Shee is the brief chronicle of James Kennelly, a strong farmer, of high reputation. The play opens on May Eve. It develops that before his marriage, many years ago, he had been bewitched by *The Linnaun Shee,* but had forsaken her, and remained faithful to Hanora, his wife. Lately, Hanora has discovered that his thoughts are again turning to the fairy woman, and she dreads the approach of May Eve, when the Linnaun is to take him away; "though, maybe, I shouldn't be blaming the fairy woman, with him these past three weeks going roaming, thinking to get a glimpse of her, or have a whisper with her, the heart breaking with him when she wouldn't answer him, and he invoking to her in the glens and the haunted places." When the Linnaun arrives, the doors springing open before her in an uncanny fashion, she appears to the others to be a horrid hag, but to Jamsie she appears as a beautiful young girl, and he goes with her. As he goes, old Denisheen Canty, who claims to have cures for every disease, slips into Jamsie's pocket a box of ointment "would give you the clear sight." "If it gave me all the sight in the world," says Jamsie, "I wouldn't rub it to them, for 'tisn't wanting I am to have taken from me my joy, let who will call it my illusion." After strange singing outside, with sudden darkness and other signs, he reappears abruptly – alone. He looks "queer and haggard," and his manner is much changed. The play ends with his reconciliation with Hanora, but it is clear that tragedy has descended on him, and that something has gone irreparably from his world.

The bond of similarity between the plays is that they deal, to a more or less thinly disguised extent, with the difficult position of the artist in a rural community. They deal with the opposition which is his usual fate, the instinctive fear and distrust of the workman, the true traditionalist, for the artist, the innovator, the destroyer of traditions. O'Shaughnessy's "musicmakers and dreamers of dreams, the movers and shakers of the wide world." There is a curious recurrent symbol in the plays. The "brown woman" who presents the magic glasses to Jaymony ("It's through a wood the brown woman came to me, and it wasn't a crackle or a noise at all she made and she walking on the grass so green. She stood for a while where the bluebells grow") reappears as the Linnaun Shee ("Twas little," says Hanora. "I knew – on the very day we were married itself – that a brown girl who was making signs to him, and laughing and smiling to him that I took to be some local having capers with him, was the dame herself, the *Linnaun Shee,* trying to draw him back to keep him with her forever") and possibly as the mermaid in *The Green Stone* ("There do be great tasby in mermaids in the month of June"). I take this symbol to be the awakening of an artistic consciousness, in opposition to the hereditary urge to settle down to "cattle and crops and all things in the agricultural way."

The characters in these plays seem to be frustrated poets, throwbacks to the great school of Gaelic poets around Sliabh Luachra, the last remnants of the old Gaelic culture. That countryside and its history are the background of the plays. The stream of Gaelic culture was broken abruptly by the flight of the Earls and the centuries of recurrent terror which followed; it was replaced by the passion for land, and the struggle to survive at any price. We survived, but the price was heavy, even more than coffin-ships jammed with emigrants, more than the loss of a language now almost dead and buried except as a patriotic fiction. The price included the strangling of creative art in rural Ireland. The potential artist is discouraged by the difference of his outlook, his entire idea of life, from that of his neighbours, which he accepts as the normal and correct attitude, in the absence of any cultural tradition to encourage him; the result, usually, is repression, frustration, near-tragedy. The loss of a potential artist is a double tragedy – for society in general, as well as for the artist himself; but Fitzmaurice's later plays have been mistakenly produced as comedies. If he had done no more than draw attention to this problem, he would have laid claim to a high reputation.

Finally, there is the sheer beauty of his dialogue, which I mentioned earlier in referring to dialect plays... "In every play that George Fitzmaurice has written," said Andrew E. Malone, "there is displayed the perfection of dialogue that delights the artist in words." "He is," said Maurice Walsh, "the best writer of Kerry dialect that Ireland has ever produced." He has Webster's faculty of making his characters say great things at high moments, a faculty which is in my opinion, the certain sign of a great writer.

WILD STRAWBERRIES

One splendid summer day twenty-five years ago there was a seaside excursion for the choir and altarboys of our village. I had actually been in the choir for one period of a few' weeks, until they tracked down the mysterious discord, but I lived almost next door to the church and therefore remained the star altarboy. So it was that in a single day I tasted for the first time coffee, ice-cream and strawberries.

I disliked all three luxuries. The coffee burned my simple country palate, the ice-cream chilled it, while the strawberries looked like jam-jar labels but seemed, unhappily, to taste the same – like labels, I mean. There wasn't a fraction of that delicate ambrosial flavour of the wild strawberries which we carried home strung on long thin blades of grass, crushing, like Tokay grapes, under their own weight.

That village in childhood was a remarkable place for wild fruit – damsons, frockens, crab-apples, elderberries (which we thought were poisonous), blackberries and strawberries. Not till long afterwards did I realise that other places weren't so well endowed. I went back some years ago, for a couple of hours, after a twenty-year absence, and found to my surprise that the little hills were just as high. There was, as always, a swarm of bees hanging from the eaves of the church, a dog asleep in the gateway, and swallows swooping over the tumbledown gravestones (where we played tig in summer to the scandal of our elders).

The school looked a bit more ramshackle, but little else had changed. Nobody recognised me anymore, yet I could, I think, have located every secret strawberry patch of my childhood. Only it was too late for strawberries, being August, and twenty years on, when my cigarette-soured palate could never have recovered those lost delights anyway.

Strawberries could be kept secret, unlike blackberries, which were a case of first come, first served. The roads were not tarred in those days, and by early summer they were several inches deep in limestone dust which spurted up between bare toes. Dust floated in a mile-long cloud behind the occasional car, and drifted down on every ditch, shrouding leaf and branch in uniform light grey. Under this veil, somewhere, strawberries were hidden. As you scuffled through the dust you tried each likely stretch of hedge, developing in the process the instincts of a truffle-hound, and when you were lucky there was an excellent chance of being lucky again the following year. Strawberry hunters were furtive and solitary.

—~—

One particular patch I discovered by sheer accident – by falling off a stile, in fact. When I had collected my wits and looked up I saw beneath a projecting stone a clump of strawberries growing from a crack in the wall. They had an incomparable flavour. And they were all mine, as long as childhood lasted.

I mentioned that clump of strawberries, casually, at the tea-table recently, and my city-reared daughter was instantly fascinated. Over and over since she has asked me to "tell us about the strawberries, Dada." I feel like something out of Ingmar Bergman, a walking myth: Dada. The Last of the Strawberry Hunters, in his grey armour of quarter-century-old limestone dust.

TERRIBLY STRANGE BEDS

I remember the first time I slept out. I had started off in a fit of enthusiasm, and with very little experience, to cycle across Europe. I hadn't even camped out before. Maybe it was as well – I didn't know what was in store for me.

That first day in France I kept cycling until very late at night and finished up in the flat country near Mary-sur-Marne, where a narrow, beautifully surfaced road runs dead straight between lines of trees through short green grass that looked as if it had been trimmed by a lawnmower. The whole place seemed so like a public park that I kept expecting a park-ranger to pop out from behind a tree and stop me from frying sausages over a Primus stove.

I had a sleeping-bag, one of those bulky ex-army items, and I unrolled it proudly for the first time and went looking for a place to sleep. I like to stretch out with my head higher than my feet so I was delighted when I found a shallow gully running parallel to the road, just beyond the trees. I spread out the bag at right angles to the gully with my feet down in the hollow, put the saddlebag under my head for a pillow and lay there looking up at the stars while I smoked a last cigarette. This, I said to myself, is the way to live. Then I turned over on my side and tried to go to sleep. The ground began to dig into my hip and the sleeping bag flapped down over my face. The night breeze began to rustle the leaves above me and every few minutes I started up, thinking it had begun to rain. Cars whizzed by on the road, their lights flashing in my face. After hours and hours of this I became so drowsy with exhaustion that I did drop off to sleep in spite of the distractions. And of course as soon as I relaxed I slid down the slope and ended up in the bottom of the gully. The heavy saddlebag rolled down after me. I had learned my first lesson.

I had plenty of time to ponder over that lesson, because the next day I ran into a young Englishman whom I'd met casually on the Channel boat. We were both heading for Switzerland and the company made the journey lighter. The trouble was that he was taking only a short trip to Lucerne with a view to further ventures the following year, while I had a long month and a round trip to Rome ahead of me. So for three days we lived at a rate appropriate to his budget. We stayed in hotels, and we dined luxuriously in station buffets (which is a lot more luxurious than it sounds to those accustomed to Irish and English railways), and once we actually took a train in order to get to our destination before nightfall. It was very pleasant, but when I was again on my own, heading southwards from Lucerne, I was brooding over the easiness of getting through a fortnight's rations in four days ... From here on, it was a case of hostels or the long acre: Swiss hotels were out of the question.

Lucerne to Andermatt doesn't look far on a map, particularly a small-scale map which doesn't show the violent wriggles of the road. Nor does it point out to the unskilled traveller that a mile uphill is equivalent to five miles on the level. As you leave Lucerne, around the shore of that incredible lake, you can see Pilatus reflected in the glassy waters. And when you look up and up and up over slopes of dull purple rock to the razor-edged, white-capped summit, it's well to remember that the white-capped summit is ten feet lower than the road over the St. Gothard Pass. But you never do remember it...

At the southern tip of the lake, the road swings away to the left, through Altdorf, past the foot of William Tell's statue, and then climbs gently towards the mountains. The slope gets steeper and steeper for ten miles or so, as far as Amsteg, and then it swings abruptly right-handed over a bridge. The bridge was my downfall – literally. After all, bridges are always on a level. They make a welcome momentary rest in a long climb. But the bridge in Amsteg goes up like the roof of a house. I practically stalled. I kicked savagely at the pedals. My incredible load of luggage began to wobble, and in a moment the whole caboodle was on the ground, with me in the middle of it. I disentangled myself, and plodded on, and the red on the back of my neck wasn't all sunburn ...

After an hour or so, and three miles progress, I came to a village with a little square and a sparkling fountain, and I stopped for ten minutes and drank a huge bottle of unexpectedly pleasant though non-alcoholic beer, described most improbably as "Blonde Hell", Then it was back to the grindstone again, with the road getting steeper all the time. I stopped again in Goschenen, and manufactured some coffee on the Primus. Goschenen is where the railway tunnel starts. No. No more trains. It also has a hostel, or so the handbook said. And it was getting dark, and it looked like rain. But on the other hand, if I did stop in Goschenen I'd never manage to get over the top of the pass the following day, and I couldn't afford the time.

I made rapid mental calculations. I had managed to struggle along so far at three miles an hour. At that rate I'd be in Andermatt in three hours, the hostel in Hospentall was only a little farther, and I'd get there before it closed. So I pushed on. Unfortunately, just out of sight of Goschenen the road began to corkscrew upwards on concrete ramps like flights of stairs, and pushing a bike though the drifts of gravel which cars and lorries had swept to the roadside was almost impossible. Twice I stopped and looked back, but I couldn't bring myself to go back down and seek out the hostel. If I once admitted defeat I might as well go straight home. I pushed on, slipping and stumbling and swearing, and travelling more and more slowly.

It grew dark – pitch dark, because there was a fine mist falling. It was very cold. A couple of times I nearly walked off the road in the darkness. Occasionally a car swished back and forth like a searchlight display as it negotiated the unseen hairpin overhead. Time went galloping damply by, and the road kept on winding upwards.

Then the road wound into a tunnel and I stopped to recover my breath, and a car came past so close that it snagged the end of a handlebar in passing, and for the second time that evening I was sitting in the roadway with all my luggage on top of me.

I looked around in a daze and saw a door-sized opening in the side of the tunnel. I thought it might be a road-mender's store, so I dragged bike and myself through the opening, and I found myself on the edge of a railway line – one of those narrow-gauge cog-and-rack railways. It was the first I'd seen, and the tracks looked like one of those toy railways in parks. There was a sloping wooden roof overhead which kept off the mist. At least I was far away from the road and in shelter. I was comparatively happy.

I dumped the bike against the rock and spread out the

sleeping bag in the only level space I could find – the sharp-edged ballast of the railway line, a yard or so away from the track. I wriggled around a bit until the sharpest stones were out of harm's way and I was reasonably comfortable. I ate an apple and I smoked a cigarette and in ten minutes I was asleep, staring up at the dark timbers of the sloping roof.

I woke suddenly after half an hour, with a horrible clanking and roaring in my ears, and I struggled to raise my head, but I was so cold that my neck wouldn't bend at first. Fortunately, for a large rugged oily collection of iron began to pass apparently a few inches above my nose. It was like a nightmare. I thought it was a nightmare. I huddled closer down into the sharp-edged stones and waited for the nightmare to pass, and when it had passed at last I saw that the nightmare was a train. Apparently the only thing narrow about a narrow- gauge train is the track itself, a useful piece of information which I had never until now possessed.

I didn't sleep again. There were trains at intervals through the night, and each of them passed a few inches above my nose. I lay there, shivering, hoping that all Swiss trains at least had the same ground-clearance. At last the morning came and I struggled out of the sleeping bag, creaking in every joint. The Primus wouldn't work, and I had lost my knife somewhere along the way, so I breakfasted on freezing cold water and chunks of stale bread, torn off crudely with my fingers and wiped on a lump of butter. Travel, they say, broadens the mind...

Eventually I got rid of the sharpest pangs of hunger, and lit my one remaining cigarette, which had been crushed into shapelessness between my ribs and the rockery. And then, with my courage somewhat restored, I packed the donkey-load back on to the bike and clambered out on to the roadway, prepared to battle bravely up the long steep miles to Andermatt. But now that it was bright broad daylight, I could see the light at the end of the tunnel no more that fifty yards away. And when I came to the end of the tunnel, I could see, two hundred yards away across a green level meadow' where summer flowers were fading, the ginger-bread houses and the cobbled streets of Andermatt. This, I realised, was the cross-roads of those great Alpine thoroughfares, the Gothard and Oberalp passes, a huge plateau that stretched all the way, like a park, from Andermatt on the eastern fringe to Hospenthal three miles away on the west. And so I had spent my cheerless night practically on the doorstep of a hostel, like a lost traveller in a snowstorm.

But the bright Sunday sun was beginning to warm my bones, and people were walking around in the narrow, winding streets. I found a cafe where I bought a handful of those little Swiss cigars, and then I sat and smoked in the growing warmth on a low wall outside the church, while I waited for Mass-time. As I sat there, the long night seemed like a bad dream, and I thought of that elegy by John Donne – "When I am gone dream me some happiness". I had plenty of moderately unpleasant experiences on that same trip as a result of sleeping abroad, including having my bike and everything else except what I stood up in stolen from beside me in Italy. As a result of that last experience, I had to hitchhike to Rome in a pair of cycling shoes which hadn't been broken in, and which succeeded in breaking me in. But even here the sleeping bag proved its worth as a sort of substitute rucksack. I put my remaining goods and chattels into it and rolled it in a bundle about three feet long, which swung from a length of webbing strap that remains my sole souvenir of that dusty little town, Parma. It was an easy bundle to carry, but I never got used to its extreme width, and I remember doing some terrible destruction in a statue shop where I had gone to ask directions. But I prefer to forget that particular episode. Nor do I really wish to remember the return journey to Paris, which I reached in a state of advanced starvation, with ninepence in my pocket.

But the proof that it wasn't all a Grimm fairy tale was that I went back again the following year and the year after, with a different bike but the same basic equipment – and the same sleeping bag. Continental hostels are all very well for somebody who intends to stay in some particular scenic district, using the hostel as headquarters. Most of the hostels seem to be in islands, or at the top of mountains. For someone who is travelling from place to place, with the object of seeing as much of the country as possible, they aren't especially useful. I make some exceptions, of course. Amboise, for instance, on an island in the Loire half-way between Tours and Orleans, one of the finest locations I've ever seen. Orleans itself, Fontainbleu, Lyons, Valence, Avignon, all these are invaluable transit points. But even the best hostel cuts down on your mobility: you travel partly for the sake of reaching a headquarters rather than for the sake of the travelling itself. And failing to reach a hostel is one of the most frustrating experiences imaginable. I know. Once when I was tired of roughing it I made up my mind to stay at the hostel in Vichy. About ten minutes after I made my decision a headwind blew up, turned into a gale, cut my speed down to a laborious crawl. I finally reached Vichy as the clocks were striking midnight, and spent two hours drowning my sorrows in a small sad cafe. And then, at 2.30, I crawled into my sleeping-bag under a tree in the park and slept quite happily until the dawn woke me with a clamour of birdsong. Better to travel carefree with no immediate destination.

Tents, of course, are a wonderful invention. For two friends and a reasonably short tour, they are ideal. In a good tent, well pitched, you can weather a three-day storm with no ill-effects beyond a few cramps from congested quarters. The trouble is that a tent must be well-pitched, which means calling a halt in the best part of the evening, when the light is fading and before the dew starts to fall, when the great pale moths go fluttering abroad and the rabbits sit on the road verges taking the evening air, when the breezes are all gone to bed and a bicycle seems to speed along by itself without conscious effort. All this is missed by the tent-dwellers. Anyhow a tent and its equipment are too much of a load for a solo traveller who believes in long-distance work. Two can share the load quite comfortably, and a two-man tent is only a few ounces heavier than a one-man shelter. But it takes a lot of tact and conciliation to stand up to the strains of life at close quarters for more than a few days at a time. Many a pair of friends have set out with high spirits and a tent and returned with lasting enmity. Solo is safest.

Once, briefly, I was almost converted to the idea of a tent, even at the disadvantage of greater weight and lessened mobility. I had a cold trip with a lot of misty days and wickedly cold nights (and it can be cold at night in June, even on the Riviera). I got back to Paris with one night of my leave left, and a bad break in the weather in sight. The hostel was full, with every inch of the floor and table already bespoken, but a friendly compatriot had a pup-tent pitched in the back yard and said I could borrow it. I got into the tent at midnight and stretched out comfortably on the deep bundle of straw which supported the sleeping bag.

It was very pleasant. There were no cold breezes to paralyse the back of the neck. The only drawback was that I couldn't see the stars, but the heavy clouds had hidden the stars in any event. Then the rain started, heavy rain with the wind behind it. I heard it battering against the canvas roof a few feet above me, and I smiled smugly at the thought of the stratagems which I had adopted to keep the wet away on less luxurious occasions. An oilskin groundsheet of doubtful water-repellancy, attached by snap-fasteners and bachelor needlework. An ancient plastic raincoat, furled uneasily around the sleeping-bag. A crackling sou'wester wrapped around my head - the first time I tried this, by the way, was with a cheap sou'wester I hadn't tested beforehand: the waterproofing hadn't worked successfully, and the oilskin was extremely slick: I didn't realise this until too late, and it cost me half an hour's profanity and some strips of skin before I could get loose the following morning. Admittedly these experiments had kept me dry and reasonably warm, but they were somewhat uncomfortable and highly ungraceful. How much better to live happily in a tent! I turned over and went to sleep. I slept soundly until two o'clock at which time I incautiously stretched out my legs, kicked the tent-pole, and brought the sodden tent down around my ears. It is a peculiarity of canvas that it will keep out any amount of rain so long as it isn't touched inside. But now that the tent was touching me all over, the accumulated arrears of rain all came through at once. I was so depressed that I made no attempt to repair the damage. I lay there in my cold bath until morning, and I made a solemn vow that not even for a circus would I enter a tent again!

No. A sleeping bag offers the possibility of rheumatism and the certainty of frequent discomfort, but it means that the sun and the stars and the wind replace the clock and the calendar, and anywhere on the map is headquarters. You can roll up your house at dawn and be on the road in ten minutes. You can travel half the night if necessary, and pitch camp in the time it takes to smoke a cigarette. Of course, in the dark you have to take pot-luck. I remember spending the night on the village green of a small place on the Cote d'Or, with the sleeping-bag stretched on what seemed to be a patch of thick, springy grass. Unfortunately the grass was neither so thick nor so springy as it seemed, and it sank down gradually to disclose that the place had apparently been used as a dumping-ground for discarded barrel bands. You will appreciate that these bands, being curved, rested on their edges. The other edge, of course, was sticking into my backbone. I spent the night digging out pieces of rusty iron and throwing them into the darkness, but there always seemed to be a replacement digging away five minutes later. They were sprouting up like mushrooms. It was near dawn by the time I finally cleared the last of the hardware and settled down to sleep. An hour later I was awakened by a loud snuffling in my ear, and opened an eye to find a dog staring at me from a finger-breadth away. He had designs on the big, crusty loaf which I was using as a present pillow and a future breakfast. Both of us were startled into immobility, but he recovered first. He snatched a mouthful of the loaf and a toothful of my ear and was away around the corner before I disentangled myself from the folds of the sleeping-bag. I finished the loaf before the rest of the coyotes came back.

I remember another night, coming back in a hurry from the neighbourhood of Bordeaux. I did about 120 miles that day, passed through Tours at midnight, and finally called a halt on the Loire towpath. I searched around for a while for a level space wide enough to hold the sleeping bag, with a small safety-margin in case I rolled over in the night, but the towpath itself was too rocky. So I crossed the road, where there was a wide level grass verge, with what looked like a sturdy hedge on the inside. I slept quite happily, tucked against the foot of the hedge. In the pale rose dawn I woke and smoked a cigarette, looked through the hedge, and was unable to move for five long minutes. The road, though I didn't know it, ran along the top of a levee. The hedge was a flimsy affair of infant shrubs. Beyond it the ground fell steeply away to a particularly unpleasant-looking swamp. One incautious movement during the night would have found me up to my neck in muck and green weeds.

Well, that's the debit side. On the credit side is the fact that, although at home I have to be dragged protesting from bed at the last possible sluggardly moment, on my Continental ramblings I couldn't help being woken at dawn. To one who sees it so rarely, the dawn has a strange fascination. The day was as long as I cared to make it. I could travel ten miles or a hundred miles with no worry about hotels or reservations. I could sleep as happily on a park bench as in a forest. I could sleep on the deck of a boat or in the corridor of a train, while less adaptable companions haggled hopelessly for berths. At least once I slept more luxuriously than in any five-star hotel. I was heading south from the Savoy Alps, and I got to the top of that curious one-sided Col de Bayard about seven o'clock. I could see the town of Gap nestling at the foot of one of those absurdly geometrical hairpin bends. I had counted my money and found that, until I cashed another cheque, I had enough money for a good dinner or a hotel, but not for both. I tossed up, and dinner won, as I had hoped. It was growing dusk when I came out of the restaurant, well-fed and well-wined, and peddled away southward. In fact, I was very well-wined, and I blamed it on the last Benedictine when I saw the first snake. Then the bicycle wheels went over another snake, and from then on I saw one about every mile of the road. They were green snakes, about eighteen inches long. They were lying on the road, quite dead. I suppose the men killed them when they were cutting hay and threw the corpses out on the road. I didn't stop to study the corpses. In Ireland we are not connoisseurs of snakes. These might be harmless grass snakes. On the other hand, they might not. How was I to prove the point, except by practical experiment? Sleeping abroad suddenly seemed not so good an idea after all. I decided to keep cycling all night, now that the moon was up and it was as bright as day. I kept it up until 3 am, and then I stopped caring about snakes, even if they were ten-foot monsters with ruby and emerald eyes. I parked the bike, fell into a drain, scrambled out of it again, and located a patch of what appeared to be tall wiry weeds. I spread the sleeping bag and crawled into it in the clear bright moonlight. The bag sank slowly on its own inner- sprung mattress, and then as the weeds crumpled the scent of lavender came floating up. I had landed myself by sheer good fortune in a bed of wild lavender. Even the noise of traffic and the thought of snakes couldn't take my delight away.

That's all history now, though I'd heartily commend it to any bachelor who is prepared to take the rough with the smooth. Now that I've given hostages to fortune, as Bacon said, I can't be meandering over the map whenever the whim takes me. The sleeping-bag, by the way, perished nobly. In the expectation of matrimony I had acquired a flat, and for the first few days I literally camped out in it. My couch consisted of the sleeping-bag spread on a mattress. I woke early one morning and smoked a cigarette. As I turned to look at the clock the flap of the sleeping-bag swung suddenly against the tip of the cigarette, and the kapok began to smoulder - a calamity which had never happened on my travels. I beat at the burning patch, and only succeeded in spreading the bonfire to several new places. Inside a minute the bag was glowing merrily in a dozen places and sending up a column of acrid smoke. I gave up the battle and dragged the bag downstairs. I threw it into the bath and turned on all the taps until my old faithful companion was merely a sodden desolate mass, wreathed in smoke and steam. A chapter had been closed. The unrecognisable remains now serve as a lagging for a friend's hot-water tank.

But no doubt some summer, in five years or ten years or twenty years, the urge and the opportunity will again recur. Out will come the tattered map of France and the well-thumbed camping catalogues. How about one of those super-de-luxe Everest sleeping-bags? Wouldn't they be the answer to many a problem? So perhaps in middle age, like that good old man Kent in King Lear, who also watched and travelled hard, "some time I will slepe out, the rest lie whistle: a good man's fortune may grow out at heels. Give you good morrow."

CAST A COLD EYE

In the morning it seemed like Siberia, and there were traces of last night's brief blizzard. Without meaning to, I managed to cut across one corner of Ballina and find myself suddenly among open white fields, so that the last and most I saw of that pleasant town was the bridge over the brown turbulent Moy. I could carry on over the hills to Dromore, or take the west coast road through Enniscrone. At tea the evening before, there had been a lady who spoke glowingly of that holiday resort, making it sound like a blend of Stockholm and Monte Carlo, so I took the left-hand road, lifting my eyes now and again to look at the cloud crawling towards me from the north.

The cloud was as black as a cat, with unpleasant sulphur-coloured streaks. Then one moment there was a signpost saying "Enniscrone – 2 miles" and the next moment the air was thick with snow. The white-capped sea, the range of sandhills that looked like the outline of the Alps south of Interlaken, were only a hundred yards away, but I could no longer see them. My world was reduced to a little wedge-shaped patch of glass where the windscreen wipers struggled valiantly like Don Quixote against the windmills.

Enniscrone, for me, was a glimpse of houses from the corner of my eye, and a peacock – a peacock! – sitting wretchedly on a gatepost while snow settled on every draggled feather. A wet hen is the conventional picture of misery, but a snow-sodden peacock is pure farce. I've always been afraid to enquire whether anyone in Enniscrone really does keep peacocks...

The snow eased off for a few minutes and away to the left, in a clump of trees, there was a tall, square, fortressy tower, outlined against the streaky curtain of a distant shower. A tall yellow tower, silhouetted against dark tumbled clouds and slanting rain – where had I seen that before? Much rummaging in my ragbag memory produced an answer: Robert Gregory's drawing of the tower, Thoor Ballylee, which the poet William Butler Yeats restored "with old mill boards and sea-green slates, and smithy work from the Gort forge." It rattled me for a while. Gort was nearly a hundred miles away to the south-west, but anything can happen in a blizzard. Here was Yeats's tower transplanted into the Yeats country where, as Jack B. Yeats put it, "all roads lead away from Sligo." The snow came billowing again and blanketed the tower like a forgotten dream, and I forged ahead through the deepening drifts towards Ballisodare. Once in a long while another car slithered past, looking like a tame avalanche.

Suddenly the road widened, came to a cross and a signpost reading: Dublin – 127 miles. The day was taking an inevitable shape. Ten miles north meant twenty' miles on the journey, perhaps the difference between getting home and stranded. On the other hand, it might be more pleasant to be stranded in Sligo than on the Alaskan highway over the Curlew Mountains – I thought for a while, then got out and tossed a halfpenny. My cold hands missed the coin on its way down and it vanished into a snowdrift. An omen anyway, if not an answer. Sligo was a street covered in brown slush, a narrow bend with a bus bearing down on me, a queue of sad-looking charabancs on the quay. Then I was out of town and still going north, determined to make the day of it. A billboard banked in snow advertised the Yeats Country Hotel. Strange how a poet and two painters symbolise a whole countryside.

Everything he wrote was read,
After certain years he won Sufficient money for his need,
Friends that have been friends indeed:
"What then?" sang Plato's ghost,
"What then?"

The billboard was one answer.

The early anthology pieces never moved me to any particular response, but the magic suddenly mastered me when I first read "1919", that strong sad simple poem: "Many ingenious lovely things are gone. That seemed sheer miracle to the multitude." Natural words in their natural order, a miracle that anyone could perform – who had the clear mind, the burning emotion, the industry and the genius. The last three years of Yeats's life alone, apart from any other work, produced 57 poems, any half-dozen of which would make a reputation for a lesser man. Yet still he searched for something more, something beyond "perfection brought".

"Have I," he asked, "that put it into words, Spoilt what old loins have sent? Eyes spiritualised by death can judge, I cannot, but I am not content." He sought the synthesis, the equivalent in literature of Einstein's achievement in expressing the world by a short line of symbols. "Infirm and aged I might stay. In some good company, I might always have hated work, Smiling at the sea – But I am not content."

It is the search itself that matters, this side of eternity.

Snow like bales of wet woolly rags coming down from where an unseen bay opened to the Arctic winds. Snow blowing from the unseen brow of Ben Bulben a few miles ahead. Snow packed inches deep on the windscreen so that the wipers struggled and finally failed, just as the gale whipped sideways at the car, which snaked and squirmed and dropped a back wheel into the ditch. I got out into the teeth of the blizzard and pushed and heaved until I got it back onto the road and started north again, sliding all over the place and keeping panic at arm's length.

A round tower loomed up suddenly and I was passing it before I spotted the sign which had lured me so far out of my way. Round a narrow bend, over a bridge, then a few houses and a crossroads with wire fences singing in the icy gale. Drumcliffe. As I aimed the car the snow stopped and the sun came slicing dazzling down over glittering white plains and diamond points of icicles on every wire and branch. Ben Bulben swept up a stone's throw away, a tremendous flatiron of snow-banded rock sailing towards Sligo Bay, with a little cloud hanging from its peak like a flag at a masthead. No wonder Yeats's early poems and plays were full of the old heroes: this was their landscape.

I went into the post office in search of a postcard, something that would conjure up the scene for me later. No, they hadn't. I might get something of the sort in Sligo. Few visitors came so far in winter.

Back to the round tower. The iron gate screeched. Around the squat ugly church, with its disproportionate steeple, the snow was undisturbed.

My feet sank in halfway to the knee as I trudged around looking for the imposing monument of my mind's eye, but always the name was wrong, the inscription too old. As I came back around the gable I saw the grave before me, so simple that I had overlooked it – a simple squarish limestone slab, the clear white letters standing out with austere dignity.

"Under Ben Bulben's head. In Drumcliffe churchyard Yeats is laid. No marble, no conventional phrase; On limestone quarried near the spot By his command these words are cut:

Cast a cold eye On life, on death,
Horseman, pass by!"

I stood there ankle-deep in snow for a few minutes, trying for the thousandth time to pin down the associations which that epitaph always set scurrying in my mind. I looked up at Ben Bulben, and saw the grim black clouds piling up behind the grim grey rocks. Time to leave the poet to his last long sleep.

The gate screeched behind me once more, and I had a hundred and fifty miles to drive in a hurry before the roads would freeze and maroon me in the Midlands that another poet made so memorable. For a while I could see in the mirror the round tower and that damp disproportionate steeple, among its few trees, then the blizzard came down and everything was shrouded over. At last, at long last, I'd visited Yeats's grave. What then, sang Plato's ghost, what then?

THE FEAST OF OVAL

Insular by definition, a green saucer, filled with brown bog, surrounded by salt sea. Geographically a nation, but often seeming more a huddle of suspicious individuals, shipwrecked mariners marooned far out in the Atlantic. "The Irish are a very fair–minded people," said Dr Johnson, "they never speak well of one another." Even our monasteries, in the great days, were more a collection of hermits' cells than a community in the European sense, and the Celts never built a town. By definition, not urbane.

We lack that sense of belonging to one another which is essential for approved public ceremonial. Events are organised by Them and attended by Us. But as private and secret individuals. We are spectators even when participants. In Rio de Janeiro and in Munich, most noticeably, and in other places of lesser note, Shrove is the sign for Carnival, for non-stop singing and dancing in the streets, for a universal orgy that submerges the individual in the group. *Carnis vale*: farewell to flesh. In Ireland, merely pancakes in the kitchen and then a tightening of the belt, calling for no public ceremony, even though Lent was the season of Ramadan-like asceticism in the memory of the young middle-aged. No butter, dry bread washed down with black tea, seven weeks of cold misery in the mists that do be rising from the bog. Ceremonies, therefore, are few and private. We children could sit in a field opposite the house, counting the saved pennies of our Lenten pocket-money and waiting for the noon Angelus on Holy Saturday. As the last strokes of the bell died away, we rushed to the village shop and bought cheap marshmallow Easter eggs in gaudy wrappers.

My father had no interest in chocolate eggs, a fact that seemed baffling to us. He was an abstemious man, whose tastes ran to bacon and cabbage rather than to more frivolous fare, but, curiously enough, Easter was the one occasion when he broke out. His private ceremony was a positive orgy of hard-boiled eggs, up to a dozen and a half at one splendid feast. Mostly he had to rely on the familiar hen's eggs, but for such an occasion he always tried to get hold of something a bit more exotic. Pullet's eggs, guinea-hen's eggs, duck eggs, even an occasional turkey egg, would join the collection.

Easter was very late that year. On Low Sunday there was already a foretaste of summer in the air, and dust was just beginning to drift on the roads. If it hadn't been Sunday I might have made the jump, in spite of maternal indignation, into my summer uniform of bare feet for the satisfaction of feeling the limestone dust squirt up between my bare toes. As it was, I had to be content with kicking at the dust where it lay deeper in the rain-worn ruts of the road, sending it up in white drifting clouds.

I passed the deserted forge, the deserted handball alley, and went on towards the stream that we called a river, which made a wide bend around the village. Even in my short lifetime I had seen progress, been made aware of change. Once only the main road had crossed the stream by a bridge. The dusty side-road, heading towards the hills where rabbits romped and frockens grew in autumn, went through a shallow ford with a shaky footbridge to one side. Here, one Christmas afternoon, I had walked with my smaller sister and my mother. We were standing in the middle of the footbridge, about to turn home again, when my sister dropped one of her new furry gloves, a present from an idolised uncle serving on a battleship in the China Sea. It teetered for a moment on the edge of the bridge and then fell in, and my mother just grabbed my sister in time to save her from following it. Helplessly we stood and watched the tiny glove, its leopardskin back looking like some curious wildfowl, bob and curtsey its way down the stream, under the trailing branches of a bush, and out of sight forever. Then for the first time, more than in the death of relatives, more even than in the sound of clods and stones battering on a coffin-lid in the old churchyard, I understood the finality of loss. Curiously, my sister doesn't even remember the occasion. Perhaps the shock was too great for her to bear and had to be fantasised, explained away. Doubtless she has her own traumas.

Children are to a surprising extent creatures of habit, and often oblivious to their surroundings. On several occasions I had walked part of the way along the bank of the stream from the other end, the main road, but the rest was as unfamiliar to me as Africa. I decided to explore it. Columbus. Last week in school we'd been told the story of how Columbus was challenged to balance an egg on one end, and had succeeded by tapping it on the table so sharply that it cracked and flattened. To me it seemed not ingenious – as the teacher obviously thought – and certainly not childish, but a pointless adult swindle.

When I climbed cautiously through the barbed wire fence at the edge of the road I thought I heard something catch and tear, but decided against investigation: perhaps

I'd only imagined it. I had enough problems, anyway, The ground here was sour and waste, overgrown with nettles and thistles, with clumps of huge blackberry bushes that cut off the view once one had clambered down from the level of the road. The stream was slow and deep and brown, with flecks of foam circling in backwaters.

I went on slowly, carefully, picking my way where the ground was driest, and soon I was around the bend and out of sight of the road, quite isolated. Here it was even more swampy and I had to jump from one tussock of rushes to the next in order to find firm footing. There was a line of scrubby alder trees here, flanking the water. Suddenly, with a frightful noise, a wood-pigeon exploded upwards in alarm from one of the trees, twigs and small feathers pattering down through the branches in its wake. I looked up, equally startled, and stepped into a quagmire so deep and glutinous that I lost one of my shoes, and had to search in the mud with my hands for long minutes before finding it. My socks were ruined. I took them off and stuffed them in my pocket and hung my shoes around my neck by their tied laces before I realised that I should have washed them in the stream, that my shirt was being covered with black mud. But it was certainly easier to walk in bare feet, even though I had to keep watching out for trailing brambles.

The stream looped away from the line of alders, where it had probably cut a new course for itself in some winter flood. What had once been a mud- bank was now a horseshoe of dense rushes, fringed by a little beach. I followed the stream instead of the trees, paddling briefly in the water, (which was still shockingly cold in spite of the sun,) to get the worst of the stinking mud off my legs. Under the overhang of the opposite bank a waterhen scurried along with that funny bobbing mechanical movement, as of a clockwork toy. I stepped out of the freezing water and into the rushes, and almost stepped into the waterhen's nest.

It was an untidy affair of weeds and bits of horsehair and sheep shearings, and one extraordinary hank of red wool thread. There were six eggs in it, surprisingly big eggs for so small a bird, brown-spotted, clumsily shaped. I squatted on my heels for a moment, looking at it, and then the bright idea struck me. I searched for my handkerchief but couldn't find it: it must have got lost when I was putting my muddy socks in my pocket. It didn't occur to me to use the socks, because they weren't clean any longer, and I had an obsession that the eggs must be kept clean and intact. I took off my jacket and laid it down, carefully transferred four of the eggs to it, then folded up the corners so as to make a sort of a bag that I could carry carefully the rest of the way, where the going became much easier all the way to the main road bridge.

There was actually a footpath here, but its pebbles were not so kind to bare feet as the dust of the by-road, so I put on my shoes again; they felt slimy and very cold. When I reached the crossroads again, I heard the chunk-chunk of a ball from the direction of the alley. There might still be time for a game before tea and somehow hurrying home with my father's Easter eggs no longer seemed so important.

Jimmy O'Connor was in the alley, practising away on his own as usual, standing near the wall and chopping the ball savagely on the half-volley, left hand, right hand, left hand, right hand. He was smaller than me, and I cherished the belief that some day I would manage to beat him, but he had more dedication to the game even if he hadn't more basic agility. I laid my folded coat carefully on top of the low wall at the back of the alley, where nobody could step on it by mistake. I lost the first game, of course, but more narrowly than usual. My hands had swelled up comfortably, become instruments of play instead of feeling, blotched and pale and cleaned of most of the mud. There was time for another game.

The ball alley was in a deplorable state, but we knew no better and had no standards of comparison. In a village with a scanty, dwindling population and little enough money for essentials, nobody bothered about maintenance, let alone repairs. We regarded the alley as an ancient monument, erected by a tribe of inconceivably remote, wealthy and powerful ancestors. The cracks and roughness in the concrete floor were familiar hazards, and we accepted as part of the game that the ball would sometimes bounce quite unpredictably. Handball, as we played it, combined chance and skill.

There was another local rule, not so important at this stage of the year, relating to the wire netting that covered the alley. This had rusted and torn in places since our ancestors had put it up, and there were large gaps in it. A ball that bounced on a crack in the floor was liable to come up at such an unexpected angle that even the most skilful could not always avoid hitting it straight up in the air and through one of these rents. There it sometimes came to rest on top of the netting, and could be dislodged by throwing stones up at it, a rather dangerous game as the wire was littered with stones left over from previous attempts, and these would come crashing down unexpectedly.

Occasionally a more violent blow would send the ball flying straight through a rent and out into the unseen field beyond, a field that would later in the year be filled with tall corn. To have any chance of recovering the ball, our unwritten rule provided that the culprit should stand absolutely still, keeping his eyes fixed on where the ball had vanished, while his partner gathered up a collection of suitable stones and brought them to him. The partner would then get out into the field and shout when prepared for observation, whereupon the stones would, one hoped, be thrown along the same line of flight and their descent observed. We became remarkably skilful at this, and though harvesting would always disclose a crop of long-lost balls, they were a small fraction of those that had been hit into the field in the course of spring and summer. That Sunday it was I, tiring, who hit the first skier. The field was so clear that Jimmy hardly needed the help of stones which I nevertheless dutifully threw, and in a moment he shouted, "Right, I've got it." I relaxed and began banging my hands together.

Then I looked around, thinking I'd see Jimmy climbing over the stile, thinking that it was getting late and we'd better hurry up and finish. Then, with a feeling of horror and no surprise at all, for somehow I knew that this was the event towards which the day had been heading. I saw him vaulting athletically over the low wall, shoulder height to us then. Inevitably, in his haste, he had placed his hand on my folded jacket.

We stood and looked at the jacket, at the mess of egg-yolk beginning to soak through it. And we could smell it. Waterhens are nervous, continually deserting their eggs through panic of one kind or another. The eggs were all addled and stinking.

We tried, hopelessly, to wash the jacket in the duck-pond at the forge, but this only made matters worse. It did nothing to remove the eggs, and less than nothing for the smell, and added some green scum to the original mixture. And then the six o'clock Angelus bell rang and I could no longer avoid going home. My handkerchief lost. Socks ruined. Shoes ruined. The trousers of my Sunday suit undeniably torn. The jacket fit only to be burned. It was no excuse that I meant well.

I don't remember too much of what followed. Trauma, by definition. "Morbid condition of body," says the dictionary, "produced by wound or external violence. Emotional shock." My father continued to enjoy his little orgy of eggs, obtained from more reliable sources than me, for many happy Easters. Not me. Eggs since then I cannot face. It's become quite easy to plead allergy since allergies became fashionable. For me Easter does not mean Carnival. *Oves vale*, rather: Farewell eggs.

A HUNTING OF THE SHARK

After years of agitation, a lamp standard had at last been erected on the corner of the quay so that fishermen could unload their catches by sight instead of touch. It was mid-winter then, twenty years ago, a raw, wretched winter. Three weeks later, at midnight, a hardy old man was leaning on the railing under the lamp when a huge bass leaped in terror from the oily water of the dock, with a great shape soaring after it. There was a clash of jaws, a sound like the launching of a lifeboat, and the smaller portion of the bass – weighing about half-a-stone – made splinters of the hard-won lamp: the rest was gone down the shark's gullet.

For the old man claimed that what he had glimpsed at the edge of the darkness wasn't a porpoise, or even a grampus, but a genuine shark such as we have often seen in South Sea films: it was twenty feet long, he said, and had jaws like a crocodile.

This was a bad business for fishermen, but even worse for a seaside resort which drew visitors by the reputation of its safe strand. There had never been sharks in Ireland, anyway. They couldn't live in cold water. Perhaps, if everyone prayed the thing might go away. And so it did.

But it came in the spring and sometimes we glimpsed a tall triangular fin slicing through the waves in the middle of the harbour. We youngsters were terrified, but also, curiously, a little proud, because we could boast of having swum in shark infested waters.

We became used to the fin, and in early summer we saw the beast himself. I suppose the warm water made him frisk. He would jump out of the water now and again and skip along on his tail, or scamper along the surface like a swan commencing flight. His speed was frightening, because water dictates its own scale of velocity, and you accept it as something immutable, like the colour of moonlight. A really fast swimmer may achieve walking pace, while the average motorboat doesn't go as fast as a cross-country runner. The 40 knots of an MTB seems almost blasphemous. Yet the shark, when he developed the playful knack of following the ferryboat, could give it a half-mile start and catch it in 50 yards, circle around it a couple of times and disappear, to emerge at the harbour mouth, miles away. Passengers on the ferryboat became very few.

Sometimes the harbour was clear for days at a time, but the tall triangular fin always came back. If the shark could be seen in the distance, standing on his tail and wagging his head like a dog begging, life went on as usual. But his submergence was the signal to finish your swimming and rush out of the water, to land your fishing boat, to delay the next sailing of the ferry.

Mr Murphy (let us call him) was coming in one morning from his motorboat in a little pram dinghy when we saw the shark coming to investigate. We shouted. Murphy made haste. The shark went out of sight. Murphy mopped his forehead and rowed gently to within twenty yards of the shore. Then the oars flew out of his hands, he fell over and his feet stuck up in the air, and the dinghy rose out of the water on the shark's nose, like the display of a balancing seal. We actually laughed.

But Murphy wasn't the man to appreciate a joke against himself and he declared war. There were many to join his army.

It isn't easy to hit a racing target from a small boat, especially if you don't know where or when the target will appear, but in the next couple of months the shark must have soaked up at least a stone of lead. He remained as friendly as ever – for it was by now clear that he was friendly – but that didn't save him from the attentions of shotguns and .22 rifles. His smooth hide began to show pale scars. Even the official marksman was hunting him, because he had done terrible destruction to nets, which he went through like so many cobwebs.

The shark's friendliness was his salvation: he usually showed himself only when there were people around, and the marksman couldn't get a safe shot. My amphibious friend, Tommy, once dived from the top of the bailiffs launch and the shark came frisking along to investigate the splash. Tommy spurted, but it was no use. There was a great commotion and he emerged sitting on the shark's back, momentarily, like Venus or Europa. Screams came from the shore, the shark departed, and Tommy struggled to land, green as seaweed, but quite undamaged.

I remember once rowing a boatload of small children back to the harbour against a strong falling tide, when over their heads I saw the shark racing towards me from the skyline. We were experts by then: I could calculate that his next upheaval would take place directly under the keel of my boat. I nearly pulled my arms from their sockets, but the tide and the load were too much for me: the episode took on the true nightmare quality of frozen action. I saw myself rescuing (perhaps) hysterical children from the waves and paying for a new boat into the bargain or, anyway, nothing less than a liner. Then I saw the shark a safe mile away, its beaky nose tilted to the sunlight, and its little eyes glittering. I hadn't time to be thankful that he had changed his tiny mind, for the children also caught sight of him, and it was only then they started screaming. I felt like drowning them.

The last time I saw the shark was on a clear morning in the following spring, when I was going back to college. Salmon yawls were putting out to sea, hugging the back-tide along the shore below the lighthouse, six men straining at the heavy sweeps in each boat. I looked back from the top of the hill and saw the shark skipping in the sunlight near the Ferry Point. He spun around, spotted the boats, and came down the harbour like an aeroplane. He surfaced just behind the last boat, put his blunt forehead against the stern, and began to push.

Instantly the men tumbled into the bottom of the boat, swept from their seats by the drag on the oars. The yawl, looking like a capsized water-beetle with its six pairs of legs waving in the air, raced ahead at thirty knots, sending out a bow-wave like a battleship. Then the shark lost interest in the game, the fishermen picked themselves up, cursing so hard I could hear them. The excitement was over. The shark, heedless of their shouts and threats, was away on the skyline, dancing gracefully on his tail around the great conical buoy that marked the harbour bar. That is how I remember him, happy and beautiful in the morning sunlight.

About a month afterwards I heard that the shark had been killed. He ventured rashly up the river as far as the bridge, where the marksman, watching for seals, had seized the chance and put five .303 bullets into the target at close range. Three days later the remains were found floating in the harbour and dragged to shore. They took a photograph, which I have still. The carcass is scarred and swollen, its beauty gone. Its wavy-banded sides are blotched by shotgun pellets, and the marksman's initials have been carved on it with a knife. The marksman himself stands proudly with one foot on his trophy. Around him are a bunch of townspeople, their faces wearing the half-hearted expressions of a formal group.

It was a dolphin, of course, and not a shark. Why did he visit us, and why did he decide to stay, in spite of cold water and hot shotguns? I do not know. I only know that I can never look across the featureless expanse of our harbour without wishing that I might suddenly see that tall triangular fin again.

A LITTLE WINTER JOURNEY

It is the nature of things that parents should die and successive generations move a step up the ladder of seniority. Aunts, however, had always seemed immortal. One of the household quintet certainly is. A few years ago she buried her husband, with lamentations that she "didn't want to live". No Hindu suttee for her, however. At the time I pointed out (not to her) the careful semantic distinction she was making in not saying she "wanted to die", and so indeed it has been. Arthritis, cataracts, heart-attacks, these she takes in her stride, and will undoubtedly outlive the Countess of Devonshire who foolishly cut short her life by falling from an apple tree at the age of 132.

Meanwhile, nesting alone in odd corners of a huge empty crumbling seaside house, like a mouse in a loaf of bread, my aunt Mina has enjoyed ill-health for the last 70 years and thereby been enabled to lead a life of much tranquillity. She is now 79 and frail and stone-deaf. It is possible that if her younger sister Lil, the only remaining member of her immediate family, should die, the shock might kill Mina, but even that is doubtful. Poor Lil has survived several broken bones, car accidents, air raids, heart attacks, suspected cancer, TB, and Parkinson's Disease, but at the end of November she was admitted to hospital with a life-expectancy from a few days to a few weeks. I felt guilty because there was so little I could do or bring myself to do for her: I couldn't even manage to write to her. My sister and I prepared to go down to Cork for her funeral at a moment's notice.

In Limerick, scene of my still-remembered schooldays, Jo and Mary had at last reached such a shaky state of health that in October they decided to give up their uncomfortable little house and retire to the City Home. No earthly reason why they shouldn't have been happy there for years, but Jo, obviously with memories of the old Workhouse days, seemed to regard it as the end of the world and sent a very gloomy letter to my sister. I felt quite confident that she would cheer up once there, relieved of the weight of responsibility which a house represents to all but the wealthy.

But I was wrong. On the Friday before Christmas there came a message that Jo had died that morning and was to be buried on Saturday. A gentle but independent creature, she had clearly just lost the desire to live and faded quietly away. I had quite liked her: she had no direct responsibility for the petty restrictions which had made my schooldays a total hell. In her honour I abandoned the tattered anorak which I'd been wearing day in, day out, for five years, in favour of an unfamiliar-feeling conventional overcoat that had been hanging up in a cleaner's bag for the same length of time. A brief spell, in terms of my accelerating middle age, whereas five miserable years in Limerick had seemed like five lifetimes.

Clearing up the usual Friday afternoon muddle in the office took longer than I expected, and it was nearly 4.30 pm when I collected my sister and set off. A wretched greasy misty day, unpleasant driving even while the light lasted and almost intolerable in the dark with the windscreen constantly obscured. Pleasantly undemanding family gossip, however, to keep my mind relaxed; the blood tie, the shared memories, the family shorthand of over forty years since we shared that high wickerwork pram in the family snap-album. When the light finally was gone we took a break while I let my eyes grow accustomed to the dark. I had a flask of strong coffee, Angela had a couple of sandwiches and some very battered biscuits. We picnicked, and talked of school holidays and school reports, of the dangers of letting kids out on bicycles in traffic that seemed normal to them but bore no relation to the empty roads of our own childhood. I remembered tangling handlebars with another boy on the way home from school and landing on our hands and knees in the middle of William Street, yet the rush-hour traffic of those days had managed to avoid us.

Thinking of Limerick, of how I hated the inoffensive (quite probably) city, had never since paused there for a moment if I had to drive through it on the way to somewhere else. I also remembered the time when Angela (who lived mostly with Mina) had been on a brief visit. It was a wet day, and as we stared out through the kitchen window in hope of a blink of sunlight I absentmindedly laid my hand on my sister's shoulder. There was a wordless banshee screech from Mary that made me jump as from an electric shock. Bashful fifteen year old that I was, even orthodox sexual associations were something future and hypothetical and more or less irrelevant in my mind, and incest was hardly even a word in the dictionary. I don't know whether Mary had actually formulated the thought in her mind, nor how nor why I could have understood her, except that the instincts in the germ-plasm simply know what the sophisticated mind may take a lifetime to learn. So I just stared at Mary, and was speechless at the filthy-mindedness of the pure in heart. I doubt whether Mary would have remembered the incident even five minutes later, certainly not for thirty years. Nor would my sister: women, even thirteen year old women, are tougher than men.

I laughed out loud, and my sister looked curiously at me, and then we recalled some thread of conversation that had been dropped ten miles back, and picked it up again and carried it through the thickening mist to Limerick, where to my surprise I automatically found the short cut that would by-pass the traffic. Much too late for even the last straggling mourners, of course: St. Munchin's Church had only a few isolated people praying, and no familiar faces. I worked out where the mortuary must be, and we went round the side of the church and found the door unlocked.

Huge high room, pale plastered walls, a trickle of light coming through from the sanctuary which was just sufficient to show the coffin on its trestles. I laid on the coffin the holly wreath which my wife had given me, and then I spent several minutes searching around for a light switch, without success. I struck a match and held it to the brass plate on Jo's coffin, and my sister and I stared at it and then at one another. The match burned my fingers and went out, and I said, "Who in the name of the sweet non-existent God IS dead?" The coffin plate said "Mary Kennedy".

Angela, just visible in the gloom, shook her head blankly, then recovered her wits and grabbed up a bunch of Mass cards and I struck more matches. All the cards referred to "Josephine" or "Johanna". I belatedly remembered the country habit of naming a family of daughters Mary Anne and Mary Kate and Mary Jane and so on, as if they were nuns, only one of whom would actually be known as Mary: not quite so bad as the wicked custom of starting off some child in a long-tailed family with the secondhand name of an elder brother or sister who had died in infancy. We had. after all, come to the right funeral.

Nothing less than the best hotel could reconcile me to Limerick. Heated to American standards, cosmopolitan in decor, it was anonymous and placeless and comforting, and I read Edmund Wilson into the small hours and then slept like a log. Up early, shaving in no hurry for once, the brilliantly lit vanity mirror showed a morning face even more like Fu Manchu than the flattering dimness of home normally revealed. Grey-green skin with deep purple grooves: and a newly missing front tooth gave me, I thought, a pleasing resemblance to Count Dracula. Nothing like knowing how the rich live.

St. Munchin's, in daylight, was seen to have gone post-Conciliar, with a forward-facing altar and a lectern instead of the old pulpit and a total absence of railings. Elegant though the effect might have been, it was rather spoiled because somebody had thrown a brown window-envelope (probably containing a Mass-offering) on the polished teak altar-surround, where it looked like a grocer's bill for God.

My brother, with whom I'd had a definitive falling-out ten years earlier, was at the other end of the pew. We nodded at each other. My sister-in-law clambered over several people to welcome me. My aunt Mary looked precisely as usual, a wiry scrap of tenacious life. My sister had thought that the shock of the death might have shattered her, but I knew better; she was always an atrocious sentimentalist, and that's a great insulator. Outside later, while we waited for everyone to be assembled, she started immediately on the childish jokes about my beard that have served her well for twenty years, and will continue to do so for another twenty-five if I live so long.

Could this be the petty tyrant who made my life so miserable? Could I have imagined it all? I looked across at the Treaty Stone. I thought of a winter morning when I had been briefly carefree and came whistling down that steep hill, round that sharp bend, cycling to school. Passing the church I had noticed that the few pedestrians were going carefully, touching the wall, and realised for the first time that I'd been cycling on a sheet of ice. Of course I fell off immediately, but in my memory it all happened in slow motion, laying me gently down flat on the glazed road while the bicycle slid on ahead, the front wheel emitting a clear keen note as it spun in air. It was, like the rest of my past, a Charlie Chaplin film in my mind, silent, flickering, having no connection with my here-and-now in which my brother, who in those days had seemed so much stronger and wiser and invulnerable and intolerably self-sufficient, was old and slow and uncertain. Time had been unkinder to him than to Mary – or even, perhaps, to me.

At length we were sorted out into groups. Angela and I gave a lift to a neighbour who had come in by early bus from what Jo and Mary had still, after fifty years absence, referred to as "home". She was a pleasant cheerful woman, and I bore her no ill-will for the occasional interminable afternoons I had spent sitting on a low wall outside her house and kicking my heels in boredom while Mary caught up with the accumulated gossip since her last trip "home". Now Jo was making her final trip in that direction, and the neighbour's prattle distracted just enough of my attention as we went in slow procession along the muddy roads. After the turn-off at Drumkeen the funeral kept on getting lost and having to stop and ask the way – to the fury of the neighbour, we being too far back in the procession to give advice, and she insisting that it wasn't going the best way in any case. But after a detour through Cappamore we eventually found the right little road to Tower Hill, the desolate little cemetery in the middle of nowhere.

No sign of a tower, and not much of a hill either, though in that flat country I suppose it counted as such: certainly one could see for miles over rain-soaked fields. It would have been a precarious trip with the coffin even in dry weather, over old graves and tumbled headstones and the remains of walls and clumps of brambles and knotted grass and lumps of slippery clay. In this weather even women carrying handbags and supporting themselves with furled umbrellas were finding difficulty keeping their footing, and the possibility of disaster with the coffin was always present. As we skirted the ruin in the centre of the graveyard we stopped for a moment and someone, invisible to me, replaced my brother on the other side of the coffin. I don't know whether he had dropped out of his own accord or whether somebody else had decided for him, but it seemed symbolical that our briefly linked arms should have been parted before the job was done. The rest of the journey was even worse, with long-lost immortelles and broken glass shades crunching underfoot, but we got safely to the furthest corner and the open grave. I felt oddly lightheaded and inexhaustible, as if I could have carried the coffin back to Limerick on my own.

The scene was so unbelievably, so perfectly typical that I wished I had brought my camera. Thin mist and sodden grass, and a scruffy little donkey grazing on the other side of a blackthorn hedge. A small ruin, being torn apart by elder trees and ivy like the buildings of Angkor, probably an old church, possibly even the "Tower", but when I asked a local man about it he just looked surprised, because it had obviously never occurred to him to wonder. A handful of mourners standing about in awkward attitudes. A feeling of expectant immobility as if the scene could be "frozen" for ever by some skilled film director.

The grave was very short, barely letting the coffin down, and it also seemed very shallow. I thought there mightn't have been time to dig it properly, but then realised that there must be rock or water to prevent it from going deeper. Because there at the head of the grave was something I hadn't seen since my days as an alter-boy in another part of the country, bringing back at once the memory of candles guttering in the breeze, of hot wax trickling down over my small hands. Tidily separated from the heaped clay were the intimations of mortality which are carefully hidden from funeral parties in more civilised places – a jumble of wood fragments, a pair of skulls, and a heap of brown bones. I edged around behind the pile of earth but couldn't get close enough without attracting attention. A pity. I would have liked to shake the hand of my grandfather who had died in 1913, and whom I had never seen. I had to content myself with casually picking up the crumbling handle of his coffin, which lay in the rubble at my feet.

The ancestral bones were reverently replaced on the new coffin, then prayers, the sprinkling of holy water, the thud of earth, some minor dramatics from Mary, and it was all over. I gave some money to the gravediggers, as my brother, moving in a sort of trance, seemed to have forgotten them. Then I had to put a new blade in the windscreen wiper and by the time that tricky little job was done I was pleasantly surprised to find that everyone else had disappeared. Surprised also to find that I had actually enjoyed the trip: will anybody have as much fun at mine? *Cabhair ní ghoirfad go gcuirtear mé i gcruinn-chomhrainn**, as O'Rahilly said long ago.

Somewhere beyond Limerick, on the Dublin road, I slashed past a car being driven slowly and carefully, and my sister recognised my brother and waved furiously but I don't know whether he saw us. I was driving fast and relaxed, in the smug confidence that my latest X-Ray was about to show something quick and fatal, a confidence that was to get me through Christmas in better humour than for years past. To a true pessimist, life is a death-sentence anyway, with no remission for good behaviour. The New Year, had I only known it, was to bring the wretched disillusion of "good news", but the New Year, like Dublin, was still a long luxurious way ahead.

THE END

"No help I'll call till I'm put in the narrow coffin"
(Translation by Thomas Kinsella)

MAURICE KENNEDY

1924 – 1992

Maurice Kennedy was born in his grandparents' house overlooking the harbour in Youghal on December 30th 1924, the middle one of three children. He spent his early years in Kildavin, County Carlow, where his mother was the village schoolmistress, but all his school holidays were spent in Youghal. Later he was educated by the Christian Brothers in Limerick, living with his father's people in term-time. He won several scholarships, including one to Cork University. After two years there reading science he lost interest and dropped out on receiving the offer of appointment as a

Junior Executive Officer in the Department of Revenue (Estate Duty Branch). He worked in Dublin as an Examiner of Estate Duties until his retirement in 1986.

Throughout his early life as a civil servant he was also a successful freelance writer, his short stories being particularly well known and widely translated. Throughout the 'fifties and 'sixties he was a regular contributor as literary and drama critic to *The Irish Times, The Irish Press* and to literary periodicals of the time. In the mid 'fifties he edited and presented a programme called Plays of the Week for RTE radio.

Kennedy married Val Mulkerns in 1953. Their children Maev, Conor, and Myles have all collaborated in the assembly of this book, which represents a small selection of his work.

www.TaraPress.net

www.ingramcontent.com/pod-product-compliance
Lightning Source LLC
Chambersburg PA
CBHW031000210726
48290CB00007B/2406

* 9 7 8 1 9 9 9 9 2 6 2 3 6 *